THE MAN NOBODY KNOWS

*By* BRUCE BARTON

# THE BOOK
# NOBODY KNOWS

Bruce Barton, who in *The Man Nobody Knows* presented Jesus with new light and force, has also interpreted the Bible for this generation. He shows why it is *worth* knowing, explains how we got it, tells what is in it, grasps its essentials, reveals its importance *to us*, portrays its great men and women in the vivid colors of *to-day*.

# *The* MAN NOBODY KNOWS

## A Discovery of the Real Jesus

By

**BRUCE BARTON**

AUTHOR OF

*What Shall It Profit a Man*

**THE BOBBS-MERRILL COMPANY
PUBLISHERS          INDIANAPOLIS**

"Wist ye not that I must be about my Father's *business?*"

6369

# CONTENTS

# HOW IT CAME TO BE WRITTEN

THE little boy's body sat bolt upright in the rough wooden chair, but his mind was very busy.

This was his weekly hour of revolt.

The kindly lady who could never seem to find her glasses would have been terribly shocked if she had known what was going on inside the little boy's mind.

"You must love Jesus," she said every Sunday, "and God."

The little boy did not say anything. He was afraid to say anything; he was almost afraid that something would happen to him because of the things he thought.

Love God! Who was always picking on people for having a good time, and sending little boys to hell because they couldn't do better in a world which he had made so hard! Why didn't God take some one his own size?

Love Jesus! The little boy looked up at the

picture which hung on the Sunday-school wall. It showed a pale young man with flabby forearms and a sad expression. The young man had red whiskers.

Then the little boy looked across to the other wall. There was Daniel, good old Daniel, standing off the lions. The little boy liked Daniel. He liked David, too, with the trusty sling that landed a stone square on the forehead of Goliath. And Moses, with his rod and his big brass snake. They were winners—those three. He wondered if David could whip Jeffries. Samson could! Say, that would have been a fight!

But Jesus! Jesus was the "lamb of God." The little boy did not know what that meant, but it sounded like Mary's little lamb. Something for girls—sissified. Jesus was also "meek and lowly," a "man of sorrows and acquainted with grief." He went around for three years telling people not to do things.

Sunday was Jesus' day; it was wrong to feel comfortable or laugh on Sunday.

# HOW IT CAME TO BE WRITTEN

The little boy was glad when the superintendent thumped the bell and announced: "We will now sing the closing hymn." One more bad hour was over. For one more week the little boy had got rid of Jesus.

Years went by and the boy grew up and became a business man.

He began to wonder about Jesus.

He said to himself: "Only strong magnetic men inspire great enthusiasm and build great organizations. Yet Jesus built the greatest organization of all. It is extraordinary."

The more sermons the man heard and the more books he read the more mystified he became.

One day he decided to wipe his mind clean of books and sermons.

He said, "I will read what the men who knew Jesus personally said about him. I will read about him as though he were a new historical character, about whom I had never heard anything at all."

# HOW IT CAME TO BE WRITTEN

The man was amazed.

A physical weakling! Where did they get that idea? Jesus pushed a plane and swung an adze; he was a successful carpenter. He slept outdoors and spent his days walking around his favorite lake. His muscles were so strong that when he drove the money-changers out, nobody dared to oppose him!

A kill-joy! He was the most popular dinner guest in Jerusalem! The criticism which proper people made was that he spent too much time with publicans and sinners (very good fellows, on the whole, the man thought) and enjoyed society too much. They called him a "wine bibber and a gluttonous man."

A failure! He picked up twelve men from the bottom ranks of business and forged them into an organization that conquered the world.

When the man had finished his reading he exclaimed, "This is a man nobody knows.

"Some day," said he, "some one will write a book about Jesus. Every business man will read it and send it to his partners and his salesmen.

For it will tell the story of the founder of modern business."

So the man waited for some one to write the book, but no one did. Instead, more books were published about the "lamb of God" who was weak and unhappy and glad to die.

The man became impatient. One day he said, "I believe I will try to write that book, myself."

And he did.

# THE MAN NOBODY KNOWS

# THE MAN
# NOBODY KNOWS

## CHAPTER I

### THE EXECUTIVE

IT WAS very late in the afternoon.

If you would like to learn the measure of a man, that is the time of day to watch him. We are all half an inch taller in the morning than at night; it is fairly easy to take a large view of things when the mind is rested and the nerves are calm. But the day is a steady drain of small annoyances, and the difference in the size of men becomes hourly more apparent. The little man loses his temper; the big man takes a firmer hold.

It was very late in the afternoon in Galilee. The dozen men who had walked all day over the dusty roads were hot and tired, and the sight of a village was very cheering, as they looked down on it from the top of a little hill. Their leader, deciding that they had gone far enough, sent two members of the party ahead to arrange for accommodations, while he and the others sat down by the roadside to wait.

After a bit the messengers were seen returning, and even at a distance it was apparent that something unpleasant had occurred. Their cheeks were flushed, their voices angry, and as they came nearer they quickened their pace, each wanting to be the first to explode the bad news. Breathlessly they told it—the people in the village had refused to receive them, had given them blunt notice to seek shelter somewhere else.

The indignation of the messengers communicated itself to the others, who at first could hardly believe their ears. This back-woods village refuse to entertain their master—it was unthinkable. He was a famous public character in that part of the world. He had healed sick people and given freely to the poor. In the

capital city crowds had followed him enthusi-
astically, so that even his disciples had become
men of importance, looked up to and talked
about. And now to have this country village
deny them admittance as its guests—

"Lord, these people are insufferable," one of
them cried. "Let us call down fire from Heav-
en and consume them."

The others joined in with enthusiasm. Fire
from Heaven—that was the idea! Make them
smart for their boorishness! Show them that
they can't affront *us* with impunity! Come,
Lord, the fire—

There are times when nothing a man can say
is nearly so powerful as saying nothing. Every
executive knows that instinctively. To argue
brings him down to the level of those with whom
he argues; silence convicts them of their folly;
they wish they had not spoken so quickly; they
wonder what he thinks. The lips of Jesus tight-
ened; his fine features showed the strain of the
preceding weeks, and in his eyes there was a
foreshadowing of the more bitter weeks to come.
He needed that night's rest, but he said not a

word. Quietly he gathered up his garments and started on, his outraged companions following. It is easy to imagine his keen disappointment. He had been working with them for three years . . . would they never catch a true vision of what he was about? He had so little time, and they were constantly wasting his time. . . . He had come to save mankind, and they wanted him to gratify his personal resentment by burning up a village!

Down the hot road they trailed after him, awed by his silence, vaguely conscious that they had failed again to measure up. "And they went to another village," says the narrative—nothing more. No debate; no bitterness; no futile conversation. In the mind of Jesus the thing was too small for comment. In a world where so much must be done, and done quickly, the memory could not afford to be burdened with a petty slight.

"And they went to another village."

Eighteen hundred years later an important

man left the White House in Washington for the War Office, with a letter from the President to the Secretary of War. In a very few minutes he was back in the White House again bursting with indignation. The President looked up in mild surprise.

"Did you give the message to Stanton?" he asked.

The other man nodded, too angry for words.

"What did he do?"

"He tore it up," exclaimed the outraged citizen, "and what's more, sir, he said you are a fool."

The President rose slowly from the desk, stretching his long frame to its full height, and regarding the wrath of the other with a quizzical glance.

"Did Stanton call me that?" he asked.

"He did, sir, and repeated it."

"Well," said the President with a dry laugh, "I reckon it must be true then, because Stanton is generally right."

The angry gentleman waited for the storm

to break, but nothing happened. Abraham Lincoln turned quietly to his desk and went on with his work. It was not the first time that he had been rebuffed. In the early months of the war when every messenger brought bad news, and no one in Washington knew at what hour the soldiers of Lee might appear at the outskirts, he had gone to call on General McClellan, taking a member of the Cabinet with him. Official etiquette prescribes that the President shall not visit a citizen, but the times were too tense for etiquette; he wanted first hand news from the only man who could give it.

The General was out, and for an hour they waited in the deserted parlor. They heard his voice at last in the hall and supposed of course that he would come in at once. But the "Young Napoleon" was too filled with his own importance; without so much as a word of greeting he brushed by, and proceeded on his haughty way up-stairs. Ten minutes passed—fifteen— half an hour—they sent a servant to remind him that the President was still waiting. Obviously shocked and embarrassed the man returned. The General was too tired for a conference, he said; he had undressed and gone to bed!

Not to make a scene before the servants, the Cabinet member restrained himself until they were on the sidewalk. Then he burst forth, demanding that this conceited upstart be removed instantly from command. Lincoln laid a soothing hand on the other's shoulder. "There, there," he said with his deep, sad smile, "I will hold McClellan's horse if only he will bring us victories."

Other leaders in history have had that superiority to personal resentment and small annoyances which is one of the surest signs of greatness; but Jesus infinitely surpasses all. He knew that pettiness brings its own punishment. The law of compensation operates inexorably to reward and afflict us by and through ourselves. The man who is mean is mean only to himself. The village that had refused to admit him required no fire; it was already dealt with. No miracles were performed in that village. No

sick were healed; no hungry were fed; no poor
received the message of encouragement and inspiration—that was the penalty for its boorishness. As for him, he forgot the incident immediately. He had work to do.

Theology has spoiled the thrill of his life by
assuming that he knew everything from the beginning—that his three years of public work
were a kind of dress rehearsal, with no real
problems or crises. What interest would there
be in such a life? What inspiration? You who
read these pages have your own creed concerning him; I have mine. Let us forget all creed
for the time being, and take the story just as
the simple narratives give it—a poor boy, grow-
ing up in a peasant family, working in a carpenter shop; gradually feeling his powers ex-
panding, beginning to have an influence over
his neighbors, recruiting a few followers, suffering disappointments and reverses, finally
death. Yet building so solidly and well that
death was only the beginning of his influence!

# THE EXECUTIVE

Stripped of all dogma this is the grandest achievement story of all! In the pages of this little book let us treat it as such. If, in so doing, we are criticized for overemphasizing the human side of his character we shall have the satisfaction of knowing that our overemphasis tends a little to offset the very great overemphasis which has been exerted on the other side. Books and books and books have been written about him as the Son of God; surely we have a reverent right to remember that his favorite title for himself was the Son of Man.

Nazareth, where he grew up, was a little town in an outlying province. In the fashionable circles of Jerusalem it was quite the thing to make fun of Nazareth—its crudities of custom and speech, its simplicity of manner. "Can any good thing come out of Nazareth?" they asked derisively when the report spread that a new prophet had arisen in that country town. The question was regarded as a complete rebuttal of his pretensions.

The Galileans were quite conscious of the city

folks' contempt, but they bore it lightly. Life
was a cheerful and easy-going affair with them.
The sun shone almost every day; the land was
fruitful; to make a living was nothing much to
worry about. There was plenty of time to visit.
Families went on picnics in Nazareth, as else-
where in the world; young people walked together in the moonlight and fell in love in the
spring. Boys laughed boisterously at their
games and got into trouble with their pranks.
And Jesus, the boy who worked in the carpenter
shop, was a leader among them.

Later on we shall refer again to those boyhood experiences, noting how they contributed
to the vigorous physique which carried him tri-
umphantly through his work. We are quite un-
mindful of chronology in writing this little book.
We are not bound by the familiar outline which
begins with the song of the angels at Bethlehem
and ends with the weeping of the women at the
cross. We shall thread our way back and forth
through the rich variety of his life, picking up
this incident and that bit of conversation, this

dramatic contact and that audacious decision, and bringing them together as best to illustrate our purpose. For that purpose is not to write a biography but to paint a portrait. So in this first chapter we pass quickly over thirty years of his life, noting only that somehow, somewhere there occurred in those years the eternal miracle—the awakening of the inner consciousness of power.

The eternal miracle! In New York one day a luncheon was tendered by a gathering of distinguished gentlemen to David Lloyd George. There were perhaps two hundred at the tables. The food was good and the speeches were impressive. But what stirred one's imagination was a study of the men at the speakers' table. There they were—some of the most influential citizens of the present-day world; and *who* were they? At one end an international financier—the son of a poor country parson. Beside him a great newspaper proprietor—he came from a tiny town in Maine and landed in New York with less than a hundred dollars. A

11

little farther along the president of a world-wide
press association—a copy boy in a country newspaper office.  And, in the center, the boy who
grew up in the poverty of an obscure Welsh
village, and became the commanding statesman
of the British Empire in the greatest crisis of
history.

When and how and where did the eternal
miracle occur in the lives of those men?  At
what hour, in the morning, in the afternoon, in
the long quiet evenings, did the audacious
thought enter the mind of each of them that he
was larger than the limits of a country town,
that his life might be bigger than his father's?
When did the thought come to Jesus?  Was it
one morning when he stood at the carpenter's
bench, the sun streaming in across the hills?
Was it late in the night, after the family had
retired, and he had slipped out to walk and
wonder under the stars?  Nobody knows.  All
we can be sure of is this—that the consciousness
of his divinity must have come to him in a time
of solitude, of awe in the presence of Nature.

# THE EXECUTIVE

The western hemisphere has been fertile in material progress, but the great religions have all come out of the East. The deserts are a symbol of the infinite; the vast spaces that divide men from the stars fill the human soul with wonder. Somewhere, at some unforgettable hour, the daring filled his heart. He knew that he was bigger than Nazareth.

Another young man had grown up near by and was beginning to be heard from in the larger world. His name was John. How much the two boys may have seen of each other we do not know; but certainly the younger, Jesus, looked up to and admired his handsome, fearless cousin. We can imagine with what eager interest he must have received the reports of John's impressive success at the capital. He was the sensation of that season. The fashionable folk of the city were flocking out to the river to hear his denunciations; some of them even accepted his demand for repentance and were baptized. His fame grew; his uncompromising speeches were quoted far and wide.

The business men of Nazareth who had been up to Jerusalem brought back stories and quotations. There was considerable head-wagging as there always is; these folk had known of John as a boy; they could hardly believe that he was as much of a man as the world seemed to think. But there was one who had no doubts. A day came when he was missing from the carpenter shop; the sensational news spread through the streets that he had gone to Jerusalem, to John, to be baptized.

John's reception of him was flattering. During the ceremony of baptism and for the rest of that day Jesus was in a state of splendid exultation. No shadow of a doubt darkened his enthusiasm. He was going to do the big things which John had done; he felt the power stirring in him; he was all eager to begin. Then the day closed and night descended, and with it came the doubts. The narrative describes them as a threefold temptation and introduces Satan to add to the dramatic quality of the event. In our simple story we need not spend much time with the description of Satan. We do not know whether he is to be regarded as a personality or as an impersonalization of an inner experience. The temptation is more real without him, more akin to our own trials and doubts. With him or without him, however, the meaning of the experience is clear.

*This* is its meaning; the day of supreme assurance had passed; the days of fearful misgiving had come. What man of outstanding genius has ever been allowed to escape them? For how many days and weeks do you think the soul of Lincoln must have been tortured? Inside himself he felt his power, but where and when would opportunity come? Must he forever ride the country circuit, and sit in a dingy office settling a community's petty disputes? Had he perhaps mistaken the inner message? Was he, after all, only a common fellow—a fair country lawyer and a good teller of jokes? Those who rode with him on the circuit testify to his terrifying moods of silence. What solemn thoughts besieged him in those silences? What fear of failure? What futile rebellion at the narrow limits of his life?

The days of Jesus' doubt are set down as forty in number. It is easy to imagine that lonely struggle. He had left a good trade among people who knew and trusted him—and for what? To become a wandering preacher, talking to folks who never heard of him? And what was he to talk about? How, with his lack of experience, should he find words for his message? Where should be begin? Who would listen? *Would* they listen? Hadn't he perhaps made a mistake? Satan, says the narrative, tempted him, saying: "You are hungry; here are stones. Make them into bread."—The temptation of material success. It was entirely unnecessary for him to be hungry *ever*. He had a good trade; he knew well enough that his organizing ability was better than Joseph's. He could build up a far more successful business and acquire comfort and wealth. Why not?

Satan comes in again, according to the narrative, taking him up into a high mountain and showing him the kingdoms of the world. "All these can be yours, if you will only compromise." He could go to Jerusalem and enter the priesthood; that was a sure road to distinction. He could do good in that way, and have the satisfaction of success as well. Or he might enter the public service, and seek political leadership. There was plenty of discontent to be capitalized, and he knew the farmer and the laborer; he was one of them; they would listen to him.

For forty days and nights the incessant fight went on, but once settled, it was settled forever. In the calm of that wilderness there came the majestic conviction which is the very soul of leadership—the faith that his spirit was linked with the Eternal, that God had sent him into the world to do a work which no one else could do, which—if he neglected it—would never be done. Magnify this temptation scene as greatly as you will; say that God spoke more clearly to him than to any who has ever lived. It is true. But to *every* man of vision the clear Voice speaks; there is no great leadership where there is not a mystic. Nothing splendid has ever been achieved except by those who dared believe that something inside themselves was superior to circumstance. To choose the sure thing is treason to the soul. . . . If this was not the meaning of the forty days in the wilderness, if Jesus did not have a *real* temptation which might have ended in his going back to the bench at Nazareth, then the forty days' struggle has no real significance to us. But the temptation *was* real, and he conquered. The youth who had been a carpenter stayed in the wilderness, a man came out. Not the full-fledged master who, within the shadow of the cross could cry, "I have overcome the world." He had still much growth to make, much progress in vision and self-confidence. But the beginnings were there. Men who looked upon him from that hour felt the authority of one who has put his spiritual house in order, and knows clearly what he is about.

Success is always exciting; we never grow tired of asking what and how. What, then, were

18

the principal elements in his power over men?
How was it that the boy from a country village
became the greatest leader?

First of all he had the voice and manner of
the leader—the personal magnetism which be-
gets loyalty and commands respect. The beginnings of it were present in him even as a boy.
John felt them. On the day when John looked
up from the river where he was baptizing converts and saw Jesus standing on the bank, he
drew back in protest. "I have need to be baptized of thee," he exclaimed, "and comest thou
to me?" The lesser man recognized the greater
instinctively. We speak of personal magnetism
as though there were something mysterious
about it—a magic quality bestowed on one in
a thousand and denied to all the rest. This is
not true. The essential element in personal
magnetism is a consuming sincerity—an overwhelming faith in the importance of the work
one has to do. Emerson said, "What you *are*
thunders so loud I can't hear what you say."
And Mirabeau, watching the face of the young

Robespierre, exclaimed, "That man will go far; he believes every word he says."

Most of us go through the world mentally divided against ourselves. We wonder whether we are in the right jobs, whether we are making the right investments, whether, after all, anything is as important as it seems to be. Our enemies are those of our own being and creation. Instinctively we wait for a commanding voice, for one who shall say authoritatively, "I have the truth. This way lies happiness and salvation." There was in Jesus supremely that quality of conviction.

Even very successful people were moved by it. Jesus had been in Jerusalem only a day or two when there came a knock at his door at night. He opened it to find Nicodemus, one of the principal men of the city; a member of the Sanhedrin, a supreme court judge. One feels the dramatic quality of the meeting—the young, almost unknown, teacher and the great man, half curious, half convinced. It would have been easy to make a mistake. Jesus might very

naturally have expressed his sense of honor at
the visit; have said: "I appreciate your coming,
sir. You are an older man and successful. I
am just starting on my work. I should like to
have you advise me as to how I may best pro-
ceed." But there was no such note in the inter-
view—no effort to make it easy for this notable
visitor to become a convert. One catches his
breath involuntarily at the audacity of the
speech:

"Verily, verily, I say to you, Nicodemus,
except you are born again you can not see the
kingdom of Heaven." And a few moments
later, "If I have told you earthly things and you
have not believed, how shall you believe if I tell
you heavenly things?"

The famous visitor did not enroll as a disciple,
was not invited to enroll; but he never forgot
the impression made by the young man's amazing self-assurance. In a few weeks the crowds
along the shores of the Sea of Galilee were to
feel the same power and respond to it. They
were quite accustomed to the discourses of the

Scribes and Pharisees—long, involved arguments backed up by many citations from the law. But this teacher was different. He quoted nobody; his own word was offered as sufficient. He taught as "one having authority and not as the scribes." Still later we have yet more striking proof of the power that supreme conviction can carry. At this date he had become so large a public influence as to threaten the peace of the rulers, and they sent a detachment of soldiers to arrest him. They were stern men, presumably immune to sentiment. They returned, after a while, empty-handed.

"What's the matter?" their commander demanded angrily. "Why didn't you bring him in?"

And they, smarting under their failure and hardly knowing how to explain it, could make only a surly excuse.

"You'll have to send some one else," they said. "We don't want to go against him. *Never man so spake.*"

They were armed; he had no defense but his

manner and tone, but these were enough. In any crowd and under any circumstances the leader stands out. By the power of his faith in himself he commands, and men instinctively obey.

This blazing conviction was the first and greatest element in the success of Jesus. The second was his wonderful power to pick men, and to recognize hidden capacities in them. It must have amazed Nicodemus when he learned the names of the twelve whom the young teacher had chosen to be his associates. What a list! Not a single well-known person on it. Nobody who had ever made a success of anything. A haphazard collection of fishermen and small-town business men, and one tax collector—a member of the most hated element in the community. What a crowd!

Nowhere is there such a startling example of executive success as the way in which that organization was brought together. Take the tax collector, Matthew, as the most striking instance. His occupation carried a heavy weight of social ostracism, but it was profitable. He was probably well-to-do according to the simple standards of the neighborhood; certainly he was a busy man and not subject to impulsive action. His addition to the group of disciples is told in a single sentence:

"And *as Jesus passed by,* he called Matthew."

Amazing. No argument; no pleading. A smaller leader would have been compelled to set up the advantages of the opportunity. "Of course you are doing well where you are and making money," he might have said. "I can't offer you as much as you are getting; in fact you may have some difficulty in making ends meet. But I think we are going to have an interesting time and shall probably accomplish a big work." Such a conversation would have been met with Matthew's reply that he would "have to think it over," and the world would never have heard his name.

There was no such trifling with Jesus. *As he passed by* he called Matthew. No executive in the world can read that sentence without acknowledging that here indeed is the Master.

24

# THE EXECUTIVE

He had the born leader's gift for seeing powers in men of which they themselves were often almost unconscious. One day as he was coming into a certain town a tremendous crowd pressed around him. There was a rich man named Zacchæus in the town; small in stature, but with such keen business ability that he had got himself generally disliked. Being curious to see the distinguished visitor he had climbed up into a tree. Imagine his surprise when Jesus stopped under the tree and commanded him to come down saying, "To-day I intend to eat at your house." The crowd was stunned. Some of the bolder spirits took it upon themselves to tell Jesus of his social blunder. He couldn't afford to make the mistake of visiting Zacchæus, they said. Their protests were without avail. They saw in Zacchæus merely a dishonest little Jew; he saw in him a man of unusual generosity and a fine sense of justice, who needed only to have those qualities revealed by some one who understood. So with Matthew—the crowd saw only a de-

25

spised tax-gatherer. Jesus saw the potential writer of a book which will live forever.

So also with that "certain Centurion," who is one of the anonymous characters in history that every business man would have liked to meet. The disciples brought him to Jesus with some misgivings and apology. They said, "Of course this man is a Roman employee, and you may reprove us for introducing him. But really he is a very good fellow, a generous man and a respecter of our faith." Jesus and the Centurion looking at each other found an immediate bond of union—each responding to the other's strength. Said the Centurion:

"Master, my servant is ill; but it is unnecessary for you to visit my house. I understand how such things are done, for I, too, am an executive; I say to this man 'Go' and he goeth; and to another 'Come,' and he cometh; and to my servant, 'Do this,' and he doeth it. Therefore, speak the word only, and I know my servant will be healed."

Jesus' face kindled with admiration. "I have

not found anywhere such faith as this," he exclaimed. This man understood him. Both were executives. They had the same problems and the same power; they talked the same language.

Having gathered together his organization, there remained for Jesus the tremendous task of training it. And herein lay the third great element in his success—his vast unending patience. The Church has attached to each of the disciples the title of Saint and thereby done most to destroy the conviction of their reality. They were very far from sainthood when he picked them up. For three years he had them with him day and night, his whole energy and resources poured out in an effort to create an understanding in them. Yet through it all they never fully understood. We have seen, at the beginning of this chapter, an example of their petulance. The narratives are full of similar discouragements.

In spite of all he could do or say, they were persuaded that he planned to overthrow the Roman power and set himself up as ruler in

Jerusalem. Hence they never tired of wrangling as to how the offices should be divided. Two of them, James and John, got their mother to come to him and ask that her sons might sit, one on his right hand and one on his left. When the other ten heard of it they were angry with James and John; but Jesus never lost his patience. He believed that the way to get faith out of men is to show that you have faith in them; and from that great principle of executive management he never wavered.

Of all the disciples Simon was most noisy and aggressive. It was he who was always volunteering advice, forever proclaiming the staunchness of his own courage and faith. One day Jesus said to him, "Before the cock crows tomorrow you will deny me thrice." Simon was indignant. Though they killed him, he cried, he would never deny! Jesus merely smiled—and that night it happened. . . . A lesser leader would have dropped Simon. "You have had your chance," he would have said, "I am sorry but I must have men around me on whom I can depend." Jesus had the rare understanding that the same man will usually not make the same mistake twice. To this frail, very human, very likable ex-fisherman he spoke no word of rebuke. Instead he played a stroke of master-strategy. "Your name is Simon," he said. "Hereafter you shall be called Peter." (A rock.) It was daring, but he knew his man. The shame of the denial had tempered the iron of that nature like fire; from that time on there was no faltering in Peter, even at the death.

The Bible presents an interesting collection of contrasts in this matter of executive ability. Samson had almost all the attributes of leadership. He was physically powerful and handsome; he had the great courage to which men always respond. No man was ever given a finer opportunity to free his countrymen from the oppressors and build up a great place of power for himself. Yet Samson failed miserably. He could do wonders singlehanded, but he could not organize. Moses started out under the same handicap. He tried to be everything and do everything; and was almost on the verge of failure. It was his father-in-law, Jethro, who saved him from calamity. Said that shrewd old man: "The thing that thou doest is not good. Thou wilt surely wear away, both thou and this people that is with thee, for this thing is too heavy for thee, for thou are not able to perform it thyself alone."

Moses took the advice and associated with himself a partner, Aaron, who was strong where he was weak. They supplemented each other and together achieved what neither of them could have done alone.

John, the Baptist, had the same lack. He could denounce, but he could not construct. He drew crowds who were willing to repent at his command, but he had no program for them after their repentance. They waited for him to organize them for some sort of effective service, and he was no organizer. So his followers drifted away and his movement gradually collapsed. The same thing might have happened to the work of Jesus. He started with much less reputation than John and a much smaller group of followers. He had only twelve, and they were untrained simple men, with elementary weakness and passions. Yet because of the fire of his personal conviction, because of his marvelous instinct for discovering their latent powers, and because of his unwavering faith and patience, he molded them into an organization which carried on victoriously. Within a very few years after his death, it was reported in a far-off corner of the Roman Empire that "these who have turned the world upside down have come hither also." A few decades later the proud Emperor himself bowed his head to the teachings of this Nazareth carpenter, transmitted through common men.

# CHAPTER II

## THE OUTDOOR MAN

To MOST of the crowd there was nothing unusual in the scene.  That is the tragedy of it.

The air was filthy with the smell of animals
and human beings herded together.  Men and
women trampled one another, crying aloud their
imprecations.  At one side of the court were the
pens of the cattle; the dove cages at the other.
In the foreground, hard-faced priests and
money-changers sat behind long tables exacting
the utmost farthing from those who came to
buy.  One would never imagine that this was
a place of worship.  Yet it was the Temple—
the center of the religious life of the nation.
And to the crowds who jammed its courts, the
spectacle seemed perfectly normal.

That was the tragedy of it.

Standing a little apart from the rest, the

young man from Nazareth watched in amazement which deepened gradually into anger. It was no familiar sight to him. He had not been in the Temple since his twelfth year, when Joseph and Mary took him up to be legally enrolled as a son of the law. His chief memory of that previous visit was of a long conversation with certain old men in a quiet room. He had not witnessed the turmoil in the outer courts, or, if he had, it made small impression on his youthful mind.

But this day was different. For weeks he had looked forward to the visit, planning the journey with a company of Galilean pilgrims who tramped all day and spent the nights in their tents under the open sky. To be sure some of the older ones muttered about the extortions of the money-changers. A woman told how the lamb which she had raised with so much devotion the previous year, had been scornfully rejected by the priests, who directed her to buy from the dealers. An old man related his experience. He had brought down the savings of months to purchase his gift, and the money-changers converted his provincial currency into the temple coin at a robber's rate. Other pilgrims had similar stories, but after all they were old people, prone to complain. The journey and the sacrifice were worth the cost. One must expect to pay for so great a privilege.

So the young man may have thought the night before; but to-day he faced the sordid reality, and his cheeks flushed. A woman's shrill tones pierced his revery like a knife; he turned to see a peasant mother protesting vainly against a ruthless exaction. An unruly animal threatened to break through the bars, and a part of the crowd fell back with cries of terror. A money-changer with the face of a pig leaned gloatingly over his hoard. . . . The young man had picked up a handful of cords from the pavement and half unconsciously now was braiding them into a whip, watching the whole scene silently.

And suddenly, without a word of warning, he strode to the table where the fat money-changer sat, and hurled it violently across the court. The startled robber lurched forward, grasping at his gains, lost his balance and fell sprawling on the ground. Another step and a second table was over-turned, and another, and another. The crowd which had melted back at the start began to catch a glimmering of what was up, and surged forward around the young man. He strode on, looking neither to right nor left. He reached the counters where the dove cages stood; with quick sure movements the cages were opened and the occupants released. Brushing aside the group of dealers who had taken their stand in front of the cattle pens, he threw down the bars and drove the bellowing animals out through the crowd and into the streets, striking vigorous blows with his little whip.

The whole thing happened so quickly that the priests were swept off their feet. Now, however, they collected themselves and bore down upon him in a body. Who was he that dared this act of defiance? Where had he come from? By what authority did he presume to interrupt their business? The crowds gave way again at the onslaught; they enjoyed the tumult as a crowd always does, and they hated the priests and robbers; but when it came to answering for the consequences, they were perfectly willing to leave it to him.

And he was willing they should. He stood flushed and panting, the little whip still in his hands. His glance swept scornfully over the faces, distorted by anger and greed.

"*This* is my authority," he cried. "It is written, 'My house shall be called a house of prayer for all the nations,' but ye have made it a den of robbers."

Stung by his taunt, his accusers hesitated, and in their moment of hesitation were lost. The soldiers turned their backs; it was nothing that they cared about. But the crowd burst forth in a mighty cheer and rushing forward bore him out of the Temple, the priests and the money-changers scurrying before him. That night his action was the talk of the town.

"Did you hear what happened in the Temple to-day?"

"Not a man of them dared stand up to him."

"Dirty thieves—it was coming to them."

"What's his name?"

"Jesus. . . . used to be a carpenter up in Nazareth."

It is a very familiar story, much preached upon and pictured. But almost invariably the pictures show him with a halo around his head, as though *that* was the explanation of his triumph. The truth is so much simpler and more impressive. There was, in his eyes, a flaming moral purpose; and greed and oppression have always shriveled before such fire. But with the majesty of his glance there was something else which counted powerfully in his favor. As his right arm rose and fell, striking its blows with that little whip, the sleeve dropped back to reveal muscles hard as iron. No one who watched him in action had any doubt that he was fully capable of taking care of himself. No flabby priest or money-changer cared to try conclusions with that arm.

There are those to whom it will seem almost irreverent to suggest that Jesus was physically strong. They think of him as a voice, a presence, a spirit; they never feel the rich contagion of his laughter, nor remember how heartily he enjoyed good food, nor think of what his years of hard toil must have done to his arms and back and legs. Look for a minute at those first thirty years.

There was no soft bed for his mother on the night he entered the world. He was brought forth in a stable, amid animals and the animal-like men who tended them. He was wrapped in rough garments and expected, almost from the beginning, to look after himself. When he was still an infant the family hurried away into Egypt. On the long trip back, some years later, he was judged old enough to walk, for there were younger children; and so, day after day, he trudged beside the little donkey, or scurried into the woods by the roadside to find fuel. It was a hard school for babyhood but it gave him a hardness that was an enormous asset later on.

# THE OUTDOOR MAN

Early in his boyhood Jesus, as the eldest son, went into the family carpenter shop. The practise of carpentry was no easy business in those simpler days. Doubtless the man who took a contract for a house assumed responsibilities for digging into the rough hillside for its foundations; for felling trees in the forest, and shaping them with an adze. In after years those who listened to the talk of Jesus by the Sea of Galilee, and heard him speak of the "man who built his house upon a rock" had no doubt that he knew what he was talking about. Some of them had seen him bending his strong clean shoulders to deliver heavy blows; or watched him trudge away into the woods, his ax over his shoulder, and return at nightfall with a rough-hewn beam.

So he "waxed strong" as the narrative tells us —a phrase which has rather been buried under the too-frequent repetition of "the meek and lowly" and "the lamb." As he grew in stature and experience he developed with his personal skill an unusual capacity for directing the work of other men so that Joseph allowed him an increasing responsibility in the management of the shop. And this was fortunate, for the day came when Joseph stood at the bench no longer —having sawed his last board, and planed it smooth—and the management of the business descended upon the shoulders of the boy who had learned it so thoroughly at his side.

Is it not high time for a larger reverence to be given to that quiet unassuming Joseph? To Mary, his wife, the church has assigned a place of eternal glory; and no thoughtful man can fail to be thankful for it. It is impossible to estimate how great an influence has been exerted for the betterment of woman's life by the fact that millions of human beings have been taught from infancy to venerate a woman. But with the glorification of Mary, there has been an almost complete neglect of Joseph. The same theology which has painted the son as soft and gentle to the point of weakness, has exalted the feminine influence in its worship, and denied any large place to the

masculine. This is partly because Mary lived
to be known and remembered by the disciples,
while nobody remembered Joseph. Was he just
an untutored peasant, married to a superior
woman, and baffled by the genius of a son whom
he could never understand? Or was there, un-
derneath his self-effacement, a vigor and faith
that molded the boy's plastic years? Was he a
happy companion to the youngsters? Did he
carry the youngest, laughing and crowing on his
shoulders from the shop? Was he full of jokes
at dinner time? Was he ever tired and short-
tempered? Did he ever punish? To all these
questions the narrative gives no answer. And
since this is so—since there is none who can re-
fute us—we have a right to form our own conception of the character of this vastly significant
and wholly unknown man, and to be guided by
the one momentous fact which we do know. It
is this. He *must* have been friendly and patient
and fine; he *must* have seemed to his children to
be an almost ideal parent—for when Jesus
sought to give mankind a new conception of the

character of God, he could find no more exalted term for his meaning than the one word "Father."

Thirty years went by. Jesus had discharged his duty; the younger children were big enough for self-support. The strange stirrings that had gone on inside him for years, setting him off more and more from his associates, were crystallized by the reports of John's success. The hour of the great decision arrived; he hung up his tools and walked out of town.

What sort of looking man was he that day when he appeared on the bank of the Jordan and applied to John for baptism? What had the thirty years of physical toil given him in stature and physique? Unfortunately the Gospel narratives supply no satisfying answer to these questions; and the only passage in ancient literature which purports to be a contemporary description of him has been proved a forgery. Nevertheless, it requires only a little reading between the lines to be sure that almost all the painters have misled us. They have shown us a frail man, under-muscled, with a soft face—a woman's face covered by a beard—and a benign but baffled look, as though the problems of living were so grievous that death would be a welcome release.

This is not the Jesus at whose word the disciples left their business to enlist in an unknown cause.

And for proof of that assertion consider only four aspects of his experience: the health that flowed out of him to create health in others; the appeal of his personality to women—weakness does not appeal to them; his lifetime of outdoor living; and the steel-like hardness of his nerves.

First, then, his power of healing.

He was teaching one day in Capernaum, in a house crowded to the doors, when a commotion occurred in the courtyard. A man sick in bed for years had heard reports of his marvelous power, and persuaded four friends to carry him to the house. Now at the very entrance their way was blocked. The eager listeners inside would not give way even to a sick man; they refused to sacrifice a single word. Sorrowfully the four friends started to carry the invalid back to his house again.

But the poor fellow's will was strong even if his body was weak. Rising on his elbow he insisted that they take him up the stairway on the outside of the house and lower him through the roof. They protested, but he was inflexible. It was his only chance for health and he would not give it up until everything had been tried. So at length they consented, and, in the midst of a sentence the teacher was interrupted dramatically; the sick man lay helpless at his feet.

Jesus stopped and bent down, taking the flabby hand in his firm grasp; his face was lighted with a wonderful smile.

"Son, thy sins are forgiven thee," he said. "Rise, take up thy bed and walk."

The sick man was stupefied. "Walk!" He had never expected to walk again. Didn't this stranger understand that he had been bedridden for years? Was this some sort of cruel jest to make him the laughing-stock of the crowd? A

44

bitter protest rushed to his lips; he started to speak and then halting himself, he looked up— up to the calm assurance of those blue eyes, the supple strength of those muscles, the ruddy skin that testifed to the rich red blood beneath—and the healing occurred! It was as though health poured out of that strong body into the weak one like electric current from a dynamo. The invalid felt the blood quicken in his palsied limbs; a faint flush crept into his thin drawn cheeks; almost involuntarily he tried to rise and found to his joy that he could!

"Walk!" Do you suppose for one minute that a weakling, uttering that syllable, would have produced any result? If the Jesus who looked down on that pitiful wreck had been the Jesus of the painters, the sick man would have dropped back with a scornful sneer and motioned his friends to carry him out. But the health of the teacher was irresistible; it seemed to cry out, "Nothing is impossible, if only your will power is strong enough." And the man who so long ago had surrendered to despair, rose and gathered up his bed and went away, healed—like hundreds of others in Galilee—by strength from an overflowing fountain of strength.

One day later, as Jesus walked in a crowd, a woman pushed forward and touched his garment; and by that single touch was cured. The witnesses acclaimed it a miracle and so it was; but we need some definition of that word. He himself was very reticent about his "miracles." It is perfectly clear that he did not interpret them in the same way that his followers did, nor attach the same importance to them. He was often reluctant to perform them, and frequently insisted that the individual who had been healed should "go and tell no man." And on one celebrated occasion—his visit to his home town, Nazareth—the narrative tells us clearly that the miraculous power was powerless, and for a very interesting and impressive reason. The people of Nazareth were his boyhood acquaintances and they were skeptical; they had heard with cynical scorn the stories of the wonders he had performed in other towns; they were determined not to be fooled; he might deceive the world, which knew him only as a teacher; but they knew him better—he was just Jesus, their old neighbor, the son of the local carpenter. So of that visit the gospel writers set down one of the most tragic sentences in literature. "He could do there no mighty work," they tell us, *"because of their unbelief."* Whatever the explanation of his miraculous power may be, it is clear that something big was required of the recipient as well as the giver. Without a belief in health on the part of the sick man, no health was forthcoming. And no man could have inspired that belief unless his own health and strength were so perfect as to make even the impossible seem easy.

Men followed him, and the leaders of men have very often been physically strong. But women worshiped him. This is significant. The names of women constitute a very large proportion of the list of his close friends. They were women from widely varying stations in life, headed by his mother. Perhaps she never fully appreciated his genius; certainly she was not without her periods of serious doubt as we shall discover later on; yet her loyalty to his best interests, as she conceived them, remained true, and she stood tearful but unwavering at the foot of the cross. There were Mary and Martha, two gentle maiden ladies who lived outside Jerusalem and in whose home with Lazarus, their brother, he enjoyed frequent hospitality; there was Joanna, a rich woman, the wife of one of Herod's stewards—these, and many others of the type which we are accustomed to designate as "good" women, followed him with a devotion which knew no weariness or fear.

The important, and too often forgotten, fact in these relationships is this—that women are *not* drawn by weakness. The sallow-faced, thin-lipped, so-called spiritual type of man may awaken maternal instinct, stirring an emotion which is half regard, half pity. But since the world began no power has fastened the affection of women upon a man like manliness. The men who have been women's men in the finest sense, have been the vital, conquering figures of history.

The other sort of women came into contact with him, too—women of less fortunate experience and reputation—whose illusions regarding men were gone, whose eyes saw piercingly, and whose lips were well-versed in phrases of contempt. As he taught in the Temple, one of them was hurried into his presence by a vulgar crowd of self-righteous Scribes and Pharisees. She had been taken in the act of infidelity, and according to the Mosaic law she could be stoned to death. Shrinking, embarrassed, yet with a look in which defiance and scorn were mingled too, she stood in his presence, and listened while their unclean lips played with the story of her shame. What thoughts must have raced through her mind—she who knew men and despised them all, and now was brought to judgment before a man! They were all alike, in her philosophy; what would this one do and say?

To her amazement, and the discomfiture of

her critics, he said nothing. He "stooped down, and with his finger wrote on the ground, as though he heard them not." They craned their necks to see what he wrote and continued to taunt him with their questions:

"Moses says stone her; what do you say?"

"Come now, if you are a prophet, here's a matter for you to decide."

"We found her in the house of So and So. She is guilty; what's *your* answer?"

All this time he had not once looked at the woman's face, and he did not look at her now. Slowly he "lifted himself up," and facing the evil-minded pack, said quietly:

"He that is without sin among you let him first cast a stone at her."

And again, says the narrative, he stooped down and wrote on the ground.

A painful silence fell upon the crowd; he continued writing. Writing what? Some have ventured the conjecture that he traced names of people and places that brought a blush of shame to men in that crowd. That may be so, but it is more impressive to think that he wrote nothing of significance; that he merely busied his finger in the sand, not to add to her discomfiture by looking in her eyes. He wrote—and one by one the thick-lipped champions of morality drew their garments around them and slipped away, until the court was empty except for him and her. Then, and only then, his glance was lifted.

"Woman, where are those thine accusers? Hath no man condemned thee?" he inquired, as if in surprise.

Amazed at the sudden turn of affairs she could hardly find her voice.

"No man, Lord," she murmured.

"Neither do I condemn thee," he answered simply. "Go, and sin no more."

From the moment when the noisy vulgar throng had broken in upon him, he was complete master of the situation. Those were men not easily abashed, but they slunk out of his presence without waiting for his command. And she, who knew men so much more truly than men ever know each other, felt his mastery, responded to his power, and spoke to him reverently as "Lord."

All his days were spent in the open air—this is the third outstanding testimony to his strength. On the Sabbath he was in the synagogue because that was where the people were gathered; but by far the greater part of his teaching was done on the shores of his lake, or in the cool recesses of the hills. He walked constantly from village to village; his face was tanned by the sun and wind. Even at night he slept outdoors, when he could—turning his back on the hot walls of the city and slipping away into the healthful freshness of the Mount of Olives. He was the type of outdoor man whom our modern thought most admires; and the vigorous activities of his days gave his nerves the strength of steel.

He stepped into a sailboat with his disciples late one afternoon, and, being very tired, lay down in the stern and was almost immediately asleep. The clouds grew thicker and the surface of the lake which had been quiet a few minutes before, was broken into sudden waves. The little boat dived and tossed, and still he slept. His disciples had grown up on the shores of that lake; they were fishermen, accustomed to its moods and not easily frightened. But they had never been out in such a storm as this. It grew fiercer; water began to come in over the side, every moment seemed to threaten destruction. At last they could stand the strain no longer; they went to the stern and woke him.

He rose without the slightest suggestion of hurry or alarm. A quick glance was enough to give him a full understanding of the situation. He issued a few quiet orders and presently the menaced boat swung round into the smoother waters of safety. Call it a miracle or not—the fact remains that it is one of the finest examples of self-control in all human history. Napoleon said that he had met few men with courage of the "two o'clock in the morning variety." Many men can be brave in the warmth of the sun and amid the heartening plaudits of the crowd; but to be wakened suddenly out of sound sleep, and then to exhibit instant mastery—that is a type of courage which is rare indeed.

Jesus had that courage, and no man ever needed it more. In the last year of his public work the forces of opposition took on a form and coherency whose significance was perfectly clear. If he refused to retreat or to compromise, there could be but one end to his career. He knew they would kill him, and he knew *how* they would kill him. More than once in his journeys he had passed the victims of the justice of that day, writhing, tortured beings nailed to crosses and waiting piteously for release. Sometimes they wilted for days before the end. The memory of such sights must have been constantly with him; at every sunset he was conscious that he had walked just one day nearer to his own ordeal.

Yet he never faltered. Calmly, cheerfully he went forward, cheering the spirits of his disciples, and striking those fiery blows against hypocrisy and oppression which were to be echoed by the hammer blows upon his cross.

And when the soldiers came to arrest him, they found him ready and still calm.

The week of his trial and crucifixion takes up a large portion of the gospels. For that week alone we can follow him almost hour by hour; we know where he ate and slept, what he said and to whom; we can trace the gathering storm of fury which finally bore him down. And this is the magnificent thing to remember—that through all that long torture of imprisonment, court trials, midnight hearings, scourgings, loss of food and loss of sleep, he never once ceased to be the master. His accusers were determined. They thronged the courtyard before the palace, clamoring for his blood, yet even they felt a momentary awe when he appeared before them on the balcony.

Even Pilate felt it. The two men offered a strange contrast standing there—the Roman governor whose lips were so soon to speak the sentence of death, and the silent, self-possessed ex-carpenter—accused and doomed—yet bearing himself with so much majesty, as though he were somehow beyond the reach of man-made law, and safe from the hurt of its penalties. In the face of the Roman were deep unpleasant lines; his cheeks were fatty with self-indulgence; he had the colorless look of indoor living. The straight young man stood inches above him, bronzed and hard, and clean as the air of his loved mountain and lake. Pilate raised his hand; the shouting and the tumult died; a deathly stillness descended upon the crowd. He turned and faced the figure at his side, and from his coarse lips there burst a sentence which is a truer portrait than any painter has ever given us. The involuntary testimony of the flabby cynical Roman in the presence of perfect strength, perfect assurance, perfect calm:

"Behold," he cried, "the man!"

# CHAPTER III

## THE SOCIABLE MAN

A WICKED falsehood has come down through the ages.

It reappeared in an English book as recently as last year. The author, in describing a visit to the high spirited Lord Fisher, tells of finding him less jovial than usual. Obviously something was weighing on his mind, and after a while he revealed it.

"You know that Pilate was succeeded as Governor of Jerusalem by Lentulus," he remarked in dull tones. . . . The new Governor gave a minute description of our Savior, concluding with the statement, *"Nobody has ever seen him laugh."*

With that wretched remark Lord Fisher lapsed into meditative silence. He wanted to be reverent; he had been well grounded in the traditions of his church and class; he would do his duty as a Christian and an Englishman, no matter what the cost. But to worship a Lord who never laughed—it was a strain. Lord Fisher made no pretense about that.

The quotation from Lentulus is a forgery, penned by an unknown impostor in a later century; yet how persistently it has lived, and with what tragic thoroughness it has done its work. How many millions of happy-minded folk, when they have thought of Jesus at all, have had a feeling of uneasiness. "Suppose," they have said, "he were to enter the room and find us laughing and enjoying ourselves! When there is so much suffering and sin in the world, is it right to be happy? What would Jesus say? . . . "

With such compunctions cheerful folk have had their brighter moments tinctured. The friendliest man who ever lived has been shut off by a black wall of tradition from those whose friendship he would most enjoy. Theology has reared a graven image, and robbed the world of the joy and laughter of the great companion.

It is not hard to understand when you remember the character of the early theologians. They lived in sad days; they were men of introspection, to whom every simple thing was symbolic of some hidden mystery; and life, itself, a tangle of philosophic formulæ.

Baffled by the death of Jesus, they rejected the splendid truth, and fashioned a creed instead. Lambs were put to death in the Temple, as a sacrifice for the sins of the worshipers; ergo, Jesus was the Lamb of God. His death had been planned from the beginning of the world; the human race was hopelessly wayward; God knew that it would be and nothing would turn Him from His vindictive purpose to destroy it but the sacrifice of an innocent Son.

. . . Thomas Paine remarked truly that no religion can be really divine which has in it any doctrine that offends the sensibilities of a little child. Is there any reader of this page whose childish sensibilities were not shocked when the traditional explanation of the death of Jesus was first poured into his ears? Would any human father, loving his children, have sentenced all to death, and been persuaded to commute the sentence only by the suffering of his best beloved?

Small wonder that the Jesus of such a doctrine was supposed never to have laughed!

The Gospels tell a different story. But the writers were men of simple minds, and naturally gave greatest emphasis to the events which impressed them most. Since death is the most dramatic of all the phenomena of life, the crucifixion and the events immediately preceding it are set forth in complete detail. The denunciation of the Pharisees (as startling to the disciples as the denunciation of the United States Senate by a barefooted philosopher would be to us); the arrest by the soldiers at night; the trial before the Sanhedrin; the hushed moment of the appearance on the balcony of Herod's palace; the long sad struggle out to Calvary, and the hours of agony on the cross—*these* were the scenes that burned themselves indelibly into their memories, and all the sunny days preceding faded into less importance. The life of Jesus, as we read it, is what the life of Lincoln would be if we were given nothing of his boyhood and young manhood, very little of his work in the White House and every detail of his assassination. All of the four gospels contain very full accounts of the weeping which attended the crucifixion—the final miracle; John alone remembered the laughter amid which the first one was performed.

It was in the little town of Cana, not far from Nazareth; and Jesus and his mother had been invited to a wedding feast. Often such a celebration continued several days. Everybody was expected to enjoy himself to the utmost as long as the food and drink lasted—and it was a point of pride with the bride's mother that both food and drink should last a long time.

Enthusiasm was at a high pitch on this occasion when a servant entered nervously and whispered a distressing message to the hostess. The wine had given out. Picture if you will the poor woman's chagrin! This was her daughter's

wedding—the one social event in the life of the
family. For it they had made every sort of
sacrifice, cutting a little from their living expenses, going without a new garment, neglect-
ing a needed repair in the house. After it was
over they could count the cost and find some
way to even up; but until the last guest had
gone, no effort should be spared to uphold the
family's dignity in the neighborhood. To this
end the poor woman had planned it in her proud
sensitive fashion; and now, at the very height
of success, the whole structure of her dreams
came tumbling down. The wine had given out.

Most of the guests were too busy to note the
entrance of the servant or the quick flush that
mounted to the hostess's cheek. But one
woman's sight and sympathy were keener. The
mother of Jesus saw every move in the little
tragedy, and with that instinct which is quicker
than reason she understood its meaning. She
leaned over to her son and confided the message
which her friendly eyes had read:

"Son, the wine is gone."

Well, what of it? He was only one of a score of guests, perhaps a hundred. There had been wine enough as it was; the party was noisy and none too restrained. Let them quiet themselves, say good-by to their hostess and get off to bed. They would feel much better for it in the morning. . . . Or, if they persisted in carrying on, let the relatives of the hostess make up the deficiency. He was only a guest from another town. Doubtless the woman's brothers were present, or, if not, then some of her neighbors. They could easily slip out and bring back wine from their own stores before the shortage was commented on. . . . Why should he be worried with what was none of his affair?

Besides, there was a precedent in the matter. Only a few weeks before when he was tortured by hunger in the wilderness, he had refused to use his miraculous power to transform stones into bread. If the recruiting of his own strength was beneath the dignity of a miracle, surely he could hardly be expected to intervene to prolong a party like this. . . . "My friends, we

have had a very pleasant evening and I am sure
we are much indebted to our hostess for it. I
think we have trespassed as far as we should
upon her generosity. I suggest that we wish the
happy couple a long and prosperous life, and
take our way home." . . . Surely this is the
solemn fashion in which a teacher ought to
talk.

Did any such thoughts cross his mind? If
they did we have no record of it. He glanced
across at the wistful face of the hostess—already
tears sparkled under her lids—he remembered
that the event was the one social triumph of her
self-sacrificing life; and instantly his decision
was formed. He sent for six pots and ordered
them filled with water. When the contents of
the first one was drawn, the ruler of the feast
lifted his glass to the bridegroom, and the bewildered but happy hostess: "Every man setteth
on first the good wine," he cried, "and when men
have drunk freely, then that which is worse; but
thou hast kept the good wine until now."

The mother of Jesus looked on in wonder.
She had never fully understood her son; she did

not ask to understand. He had somehow saved the situation; she did not question how. And what was sufficient for her, is sufficient for us. The whole problem of his "miracles" is beyond our arguments, at this distance. We either accept them or reject them according to the make-up of our minds. But if they are to be accepted at all, then surely this first one ought not to be omitted. It often *is* omitted from the comments on his life, or at least passed over hastily. But to us who think first of his friendliness, it seems gloriously characteristic, setting the pattern for all the three years that were to follow. "I came that ye might have life," he exclaimed, "and have it more abundantly." So, at the very outset, he makes use of his mighty power, not to point a solemn moral, not to relieve a sufferer's pain, but to keep a happy party from breaking up too soon, to save a hostess from embarrassment. . . . See, the ruler of the feast rises to propose a toast . . . hark to the discordant strains of the neighborhood orchestra . . . look, a tall broad-shouldered man towers above the crowd . . . listen, hear his laugh!

The Jewish prophets were stern-faced men; there are few if any gleams of humor in the Old Testament from beginning to end. It was the business of a prophet to denounce folks for their sins. Go to the Boston Public Library and look at their portraits. You are moved by their moral grandeur, but rather glad to get away. They are not the kind of men whom you would choose as companions on a fishing trip.

John the Baptist was the last of this majestic succession of thunderers. He forsook the cities as being wicked beyond any hope, and pitched his camp in a wilderness beside the banks of the Jordan. For clothes he wore the skins of animals; his food was locusts and wild honey. He indulged in long fasts and vigils, from which he emerged with flaming eyeballs to deliver his uncompromising challenge. "Repent," he cried, stretching out his gaunt arm toward the thoughtless capital, "repent while you still have time. God has given up hope. His patience is exhausted; He is about to wind up the affairs of the world." Many people flocked out to his camp and his fiery language burned through to consciences that were overgrown with a very thick crust.

Fresh from the carpenter shop came Jesus to stand and listen with the rest. To what degree was he influenced? Did he, too, believe that the world was almost at an end? Did he see himself cast in a role like John's, a voice in the wilderness, crying destruction? There is some evidence to make us think so. He went away from John's camp and hid himself in the woods, and there for forty days and nights he fought the thing through. But at the end his mind was made up. His place was among his fellows. For a time his preaching bore a decided resemblance to John's. He, too, talked of the imminence of the Kingdom of Heaven and warned his hearers that time was short. But little by little the note of warning diminished; the appeal to righteousness as a happier, more satisfying way of living increased. God ceased to be the stern, unforgiving judge, and became the loving, friendly Father. He, himself, was less and less the prophet, more and more the companion. So much so, that John—imprisoned and depressed—began to be tortured by doubt. Was this Jesus really the man whom he had hoped would carry on his work? Had he, John, made a mistake? What were these rumors that came to him of Jesus' conduct—his presence at parties, his failure to keep the stipulated fasts, the unconventional habits of his followers? What did such unprophetic conduct mean?

John sent two of his disciples to watch and to ask. And Jesus, knowing how wide was the difference between their attitude and his, refused to argue or defend. "Go and tell your master what you have seen and heard," he said. "The sick are healed, the blind receive their sight and the poor have the gospel preached to them. . . . It is true that I do not fast, nor forego the every-day pleasures of life. John did his work and it was fine; but I can not work in his way. I must be myself . . . and these results which you have seen . . . these are my evidence."

He loved to be in the crowd. Apparently he

attended all the feasts at Jerusalem not merely as religious festivals but because all the folks were there and he had an all-embracing fondness for folks. We err if we think of him as a social outsider. To be sure it was the "poor" who "heard him gladly," and most of his close disciples were men and women of the lower classes. But there was a time when he was quite the favorite in Jerusalem. The story of his days is dotted with these phrases. . . . "A certain ruler desired him that he should eat with him." . . . . "They desired him greatly to remain and he abode two days." . . . . Even after he had denounced the Pharisees as "hypocrites" and "children of the devil," even when the clouds of disapproval were gathering for the final storm, they still could not resist the charm of his presence, nor the stimulation of his talk. Close up to the end of the story we read that a "certain chief of the Pharisees desired him that he would dine at his house."

No other public character ever had a more interesting list of friends. It ran from the top of the social ladder to the bottom. Nicodemus, the member of the supreme court, had too big a stake in the social order to dare to be a disciple, but he was friendly all the way through, and notably at the end. Some unknown rich man, the owner of an estate on the Mount of Olives, threw it open to Jesus gladly as a place of retirement and rest. When he needed a room for the last supper with his friends he had only to send a messenger ahead and ask for it. The request was enough. A Roman centurion was glad to be counted among his acquaintances; the wife of the steward of Herod, and probably the steward himself, contributed to his comfort. And in the last sad hours, when the hatred of his enemies had completed its work and his body hung lifeless from the cross, it was a rich man named Joseph—a rich man who would have sunk into oblivion like the other rich men of all the ages except for this one great act of friendship—who begged the authorities for his body, and having prepared it for burial laid it in a private tomb.

Such were his associates among the socially elect. What sort of people made up the rest of his circle? All sorts. Pharisees, fishermen; merchants and tax collectors; cultivated women and outcast women; soldiers, lawyers, beggars, lepers, publicans and sinners. What a spectacle they must have presented trailing after him through the streets, or covering the side of the green slopes of the mountain where he delivered his one long discourse! How they reveled in the keen thrust of his answers, when some smart member of the company tried to trip him up. What heated arguments carried back and forth; what shrewd retorts, what pointed jokes! He loved it all—the pressure of the crowd, the clash of wits, the eating and the after-dinner talk. When he was criticized *because* he enjoyed it so much and because his disciples did not fast and go about with gloomy looks, he gave an answer that throws a wonderful light upon his own conception of his mission.

"Do the friends of the bridegroom fast while the bridegroom is still with them?" he demanded. "Not a bit of it; they enjoy every moment of his stay. I am the bridegroom; these are my hours of celebration. Let my friends be happy with me for the little while that we are together. There will be plenty of time for solemn thoughts after I am gone."

This was his own picture of himself—a bridegroom! The center and soul of a glorious existence; a bringer of news so wonderful that those who received it should be marked by their radiance as by a badge. Of course he disregarded the narrow code of the Pharisees.

"You shall walk only so far on the Sabbath," said the Code. He walked as far as he liked.

"These things you may eat and these you shall not," said the Code.

"You're not defiled by what goes into your mouth," he answered, "but by what comes out."

"All prayers must be submitted according to the forms provided," said the Code. "None others are acceptable."

It was blasphemy to him. His God was no Bureau, no Rule Maker, no Accountant. "God is a spirit," he cried. "Between the great Spirit and the spirits of men—which are a tiny part of His—no one has the right to intervene with formulæ and rules."

He told a story which must have outraged the self-righteous members of his audience. He said that a certain man had two sons. The elder, a perfectly proper and perfectly uninteresting young man, worked hard, saved his money, and conducted himself generally as a respectable member of society. But people were gloomier rather than happier when he came around. He never once gave way to a generous impulse.

The younger son was a reckless ne'er-do-well, who took his portion of the estate and went into a far country where he led a wild life and presently was penniless and repentant. In that mood he proceeded to work his way back to his father's house. The father had never ceased to watch and hope; he saw the boy coming a long way down the road, ran to him, threw his arms around his dusty shoulders, kissed his forehead, and bore him in triumph to the front door.

"Bring a fatted calf," he cried. "Make a feast; call the neighbors in to celebrate. For this my son which was gone has come back; he was dead to decency and idealism. Now he has cleaned up his thinking and is alive again."

There were high doings in that house that day, and every one enjoyed them except the older son. He was sullen and self-pitying. "Where do I come in?" he exclaimed. "Here I work and save and have never had a good time. This irresponsible youngster has had nothing but good times and now, when he comes home after having run through his money, they give him a party. It's wrong."

The father did not defend the younger son, but he *rebuked* the elder. That was what hurt the smugly complacent members of the audience to whom Jesus told the story. The implication was too plain. "There are two ways in which a man may waste his life," the story said in effect. "One is to run away from your responsibilities, causing sorrow to your parents and hurt to your associates, killing your finer na-

ture.  That is wrong, and a man must repent
of such conduct and change his life if he is to
be received again into his Father's house.

"But the other thing is equally wrong.  God
is a generous Giver, and selfish getting is sin.
God laughs in the sunshine and sings through
the throats of birds.  They who neither laugh
nor sing are out of tune with the Infinite.  God
has exercised all his ingenuity in making the
world a pleasant place.  Those who find no
pleasure and give none offer Him a constant affront.  However precise their conduct, their
spirits are an offense. . . . Woe to you, Scribes
and Pharisees.  You are painfully careful to
give exactly one-tenth of your incomes to the
Temple, figuring down to fractions of pennies.
But you neglect the weightier matters of the
law—the supreme obligation to leave the world
a little more cheerful because you have passed
through."

This was his message—a happy God, wanting
His sons and daughters to be happy.

Jesus grew tremendously sure of himself as

his ministry progressed. No passages in all literature are more scathing than his denunciations of the cheerless, self-righteous Pharisees. They smarted under the sting, and the crowds laughed at their discomfiture and cheered the young man who dared to call himself the greatest of the prophets and still proclaimed that life is a gift to be enjoyed, not a penance to be served. All achieving characters have a sublime disregard of criticism. "Never explain; never retract; never apologize; get it done and let them howl," was the motto of a great Englishman. It might well have been the motto of Jesus. "No man can expect to accomplish anything if he stands in terror of public opinion," he said in substance. "People will talk against you no matter how you live or what you do. Look at John the Baptist. He came neither eating nor drinking and they said he had a devil. I come both eating and drinking, and what do they call me? A wine bibber and a gluttonous man!"

He must have told it as a joke on himself and on John, though the Gospels do not say so. In-

deed we must often wonder how much of his
humor has been lost to us by the literal minded-
ness of his chroniclers. How about that incident, for example, at the pool of Bethesda? The
pool was in Jerusalem near the sheep market
and was supposed to have magic properties.
Hundreds of sick people were left along the
edges to wait for the moment when the waters
would be stirred by the visit of an angel from
Heaven; whoever managed to get into the water
first, after the stirring, was healed. Passing by
it one afternoon Jesus heard the whining voice
of an old fellow who had been lying there for
thirty-eight years. Every time the pool stirred,
he made a half-hearted effort to jump in; but
there was always some one with more determination, or more helpful friends. So the old chap
would drop back on to his couch and bemoan his
hard luck. He was bemoaning it on this day
when Jesus stopped and looked at him with a
whimsical smile.

"Wilt thou be made whole?" Jesus demanded.

The old man was instantly resentful. What

an absurd question! Of course he wanted to be made whole! Hadn't he been trying for thirty-eight years? Why annoy him with such an impertinence?

The smile on the face of Jesus broadened. He knew better. Enjoying poor health was the old fellow's profession. He was a marked man in those parts; in the daily grumblings, when the sufferers aired their complaints, he was the principal speaker. Nobody had as many pains as he; no other symptoms were so distressing. Let these newcomers take a back seat. His was the only original hard luck story. He had been there for thirty-eight years.

The keen eyes of Jesus saw deep into the souls of men. There was a twinkle in them now:

"Get up," he said briskly, "and walk."

The old chap spluttered and grumbled, but there was no resisting the command of that presence. He rose, discovered to his own amazement that he could stand, rolled up his bed and moved off. A reverent hush fell on the assembled crowd, and before they could find their voices Jesus, too, was gone. The disciples were too deeply impressed for comment; they dropped back a respectful distance and Jesus walked on alone. Suppose they had followed closer? Wouldn't their ears have been startled by something suspiciously like a chuckle? . . . It was a good joke on the old chap. He imagined that he'd had hard luck, but his real hard luck was just beginning. . . . No more of the pleasure of self-pity for him. . . . What would his folks say that night when he came walking in? . . . What a shock to him in the morning when they told him that he'd have to go to work!

The shortest verse in the New Testament is "Jesus wept." That tragic note in his story the Gospel record has carefully preserved. How we wish it might also have told us what occurred on the night after the chronic old grumbler was healed. Did Jesus stop suddenly in the middle of the supper, and set down his cup, while a broad smile spread across his wonderful face? If he did the disciples were probably puzzled— they were so often puzzled— but surely we have the reverent right to guess what was in his mind, as he pictured the home-coming of that cured old man. On that evening surely Jesus *must* have laughed.

Some one has said that genius is the ability to become a boy again at will. Lincoln had that type of genius. Around his table in Washington sat the members of his Cabinet silenced by their overwhelming sense of responsibility. It was one of the most momentous meetings in our history. To their amazement instead of addressing himself directly to the business in hand, Lincoln picked up a volume and began to read aloud a delightful chapter of nonsense from Artemus Ward.

Frequent chuckles interrupted the reading, but they came only from the President. The Secretaries were too shocked for expression! Humor at such an hour—it was well nigh sacrilegious! Heedless of their protesting looks, Lincoln finished the chapter, closed the book and scanned their gloomy faces with a sigh.

"Gentlemen, why don't you laugh?" he exclaimed. "With the fearful strain that is upon me night and day, if I did not laugh I should die; and you need this medicine as much as I."

With that remark he turned to his tall hat which was on the table and drew forth what Secretary Stanton described as a "little white paper."

The "little white paper" was the Emancipation Proclamation.

Stanton could scarcely restrain his impulse to stalk out of the room. No one of his Cabinet really understood Lincoln. He was constantly scandalizing them by his calm disregard of convention, and his seemingly prodigal waste of time. The friends and advisers of Jesus were similarly shocked. How could any one with such important business allow himself to be so casually interrupted! One of the surest marks of greatness, of course, is accessibility and the appearance of having an unstinted allowance of time. "Extreme busyness is a symptom of deficient vitality," says Stevenson. The disciples were extremely busy, Judas most of all. He was the treasurer of the group, harassed because expenses ran high and there was no certainty of to-morrow's income. Jesus brushed away such petty worries with a smile.

"Consider the lilies of the field," he exclaimed, "they toil not neither do they spin, yet Solomon in all his glory was not arrayed like one of these." That was all very poetic, very nice, but it did not fool Judas. He knew that you can not get anywhere in the world without money and it was his job to find the money. The other disciples had similar worries. They wanted to get it clear as to their relative positions in the new Kingdom; they were concerned because outsiders, not properly initiated into the organization, were claiming to be followers of Jesus and doing miracles in his name. They fretted because there was so much work to be done and the days too short for doing it.

But he towered magnificently above it all. Wherever he went the children flocked. Pomp and circumstances mean nothing to them. They are neither attracted by prominence nor awed in its presence. Their instinct cuts through all outward semblance with a keen swift edge; unfailingly they comprehend who are real and who are not. With a knowledge which is the accumulated wisdom of all the ages they recognize their friends.

So they swarmed around, climbing on his knees, tugging at his garments, smiling up into his eyes, begging to hear more of his stories. It was all highly improper and wasteful in the disciples' eyes. With bustling efficiency they hastened to remind him that he had important appointments; tried to push eager mothers back.

But Jesus would have none of it. "Suffer the little children to come unto me!" he commanded. And he added one of those sayings which should make so clear the message of his gospel. "They are the very essence of the Kingdom of Heaven," he said, "unless you become like them you shall in no wise enter in." Like them . . . like little children . . . laughing . . . joyous . . . unaffected . . . trusting implicitly . . . with time to be kind.

To be sure he was not always in the crowd. He had his long hours of withdrawal when, in communion with his Father, he refilled the deep reservoirs of his strength and love. Toward the end he was more preoccupied. He knew months in advance that if he made another journey to Jerusalem his fate would be sealed; yet he never wavered in his decision to make that journey. Starting out on it, his mind filled with the approaching conflict, his shoulders burdened with the whole world's need, he heard his name called out from the roadside in shrill unfamiliar tones. "Jesus . . . Jesus . . . thou son of David . . . have mercy on me."

It was the voice of a useless blind beggar. . . . At once the disciples were upon him, commanding silence. Couldn't he see that the Master was deep in thought? Who was he to interrupt. . . . Keep still, blind man . . . get back where you belong. . . .

But frantic hope knows no reserve. It was the poor fellow's one possible chance. . . . He cared no more for their rebuke than they for his need. Again the shrill insistent voice: "Jesus, thou son of David, have mercy on me."

Jesus stopped.

"Who called my name?"

"Nobody, Master . . . only a blind beggar . . . a worthless fellow . . . Bartimæus . . . nobody at all . . . we'll tend to him."

"Bring him here."

Trembling with hope he was guided forward. The deep rich eyes of the Master looked into those sightless eyes. The mind which had been buried in the greatest problem with which a mind ever wrestled, gave itself unreservedly to the problem of one forlorn human life. Here was need; and *he* had time. . . .

Something more than a hundred years ago a sermon was preached in St. John's Church, New York, which dealt very severely with the frailties of poor human nature, and put forth, with unctuous assurance, the promise of eternal punishment for a large proportion of the race. Among the worshipers was a gentleman of unfortunate reputation but keen mind, whose name lingers unforgettably in our history. As he left the church a lady spoke to him:

"What did you think of the sermon, Mr. Burr?" she asked.

"I think," responded Aaron Burr, "that God is better than most people suppose."

That was the message of Jesus—that God is supremely better than anybody had ever dared to believe. Not a petulant Creator, who had lost control of his creation and, in wrath, was determined to destroy it all. Not a stern Judge dispensing impersonal justice. Not a vain King who must be flattered and bribed into concessions of mercy. Not a rigid Accountant, checking up the sins against the penances and striking a cold hard balance. Not any of these . . . nothing like these . . . but a great Companion, a wonderful Friend, a kindly indulgent, joy-loving Father. . . .

For three years Jesus walked up and down the shores of his lake and through the streets of towns and cities, trying to make them understand. Then came the end, and almost before

his fine firm flesh was cold, the distortion began.
He who had cared nothing for ceremonies and
forms was made the idol of formalism. Men hid
themselves in monasteries; they lashed themselves with whips; they tortured their skins with
harsh garments and cried out that they were followers of him—of *him* who loved the crowd,
who gathered children about him wherever he
went, who celebrated the calling of a new disciple with a feast in which all the neighborhood
joined! "Hold your heads high," he had exclaimed, "you are lords of the universe . . .
only a little lower than the angels . . . children
of God." But the hymn writers knew better.
They wrote:

> "Oh to be *nothing, nothing*"

and

> "For such a *worm* as I."

His last supper with his disciples was an hour of
solemn memories. Their minds were heavy with
foreboding. He talked earnestly, but the whole

purpose of his talk was to lift up their hearts, to make them think nobly of themselves, to fill their spirits with a conquering faith.

"My joy I leave with you," he exclaimed.

"Be of good cheer," he exclaimed.

Joy . . . cheer . . . these are the words by which he wished to be remembered. But down through the ages has come the wicked falsehood that he never laughed.

# CHAPTER IV

## HIS METHOD

MANY leaders have dared to lay out ambitious programs, but this is the most daring of all:

"Go ye into all the world," Jesus said, "and preach the gospel *to the whole creation*."

Consider the sublime audacity of that command. To carry Roman civilization across the then known world had cost millions of lives and billions in treasure. To create any sort of reception for a new idea or product to-day involves a vast machinery of propaganda and expense. Jesus had no funds and no machinery. His organization was a tiny group of uneducated men, one of whom had already abandoned the cause as hopeless, deserting to the enemy. He had come proclaiming a Kingdom and was to end upon a cross; yet he dared to talk of conquering all creation. What was the source of his faith in that handful of followers? By what methods had he trained them? What had they learned from him of the secrets of influencing men?

We speak of the law of "supply and demand," but the words have got turned around. With anything which is not a basic necessity the supply always precedes the demand. Elias Howe invented the sewing machine, but it nearly rusted away before American women could be persuaded to use it. With their sewing finished so quickly what would they ever do with their spare time? Howe had vision, and had made his vision come true; but he could not sell! So his biographer paints a tragic picture—the man who had done more than any other in his generation to lighten the labor of women is forced to attend the funeral of the woman he loved in a borrowed suit of clothes! Nor are men less stubborn than women in opposition to the new idea. The typewriter had been a demonstrated success for years before business men could be persuaded to buy it. How could any

one have letters enough to justify the investment of one hundred dollars in a writing machine? Only when the Remingtons sold the
Caligraph Company the right to manufacture
machines under the Remington patent, and two
groups of salesmen set forth in competition, was
the resistance broken down.

Almost every invention has had a similar battle. Said Robert Fulton of the *Clermont:*

"As I had occasion daily to pass to and from
the shipyard where my boat was in progress, I
often loitered near the groups of strangers and
heard various inquiries as to the object of this
new vehicle. The language was uniformly that
of scorn, sneer or ridicule. The loud laugh often
rose at my expense; the dry jest; the wise cal-
culations of losses or expenditures; the dull
repetition of 'Fulton's Folly.' Never did a
single encouraging remark, a bright hope, a
warm wish cross my path."

That is the kind of human beings we are—
wise in our own conceit, impervious to sugges-
tions, perfectly sure that what's never been done

never will be done. Nineteen hundred years ago
we were even more impenetrable, for modern
science has frequently shot through the hard
shell of our complacency. . . . *"To the whole
creation."* . . . Assuredly there was no demand
for a new religion; the world was already over-
supplied. And Jesus proposed to send forth
eleven men and expect them to substitute his
thinking for all existing religious thought!

In this great act of courage he was the successor, and the surpasser, of all the prophets
who had gone before. We spoke a moment ago
of the prophets as deficient in humor; but what
they lacked in the amenities of life they made up
richly in vision. Each one of them brought to
the world a revolutionary idea, and we can not
understand truly the significance of the work of
Jesus unless we remember that he began where
they left off, building on the firm foundations
they had laid. Let us glance at them a moment,
starting with Moses. What a miracle he
wrought in the thinking of his race! The world
was full of gods in his day—male gods, female

gods, wooden and iron gods—it was a poverty stricken tribe which could not boast of a hundred at least. The human mind had never been able to leap beyond the idea that every natural phenomenon was the expression of a different deity. Along came Moses with one of the transcendent intellects of history. "There is one God," he cried. What an overwhelming idea and how magnificent its consequences. Taking a disorganized crowd of folks who had been slaves in Egypt for generations—their spirits broken by rule and rod—Moses persuaded them that God, this one all-powerful God, was their special friend and protector, fired them with faith in that conviction and transformed them from slaves to conquerors!

Moses died and the nation carried on under the momentum which he had given it, until there arose Amos, a worthy successor.

"There is one God," Moses had said.

"God is a God of justice," added Amos.

That assertion is such an elementary part of our consciousness that we are almost shocked by

the suggestion that it could ever have been new.
But remember the gods that were current in
Amos's day if you would have a true measure
of the importance of his contribution—the gods
of the Greeks, for example. Zeus was chief of
them, a philandering old reprobate who visited
his wrath upon such mortals as were unlucky
enough to interfere in his love affairs, and threw
his influence to whichever side offered the larg-
est bribes. His wife and sons and daughters
were no better; nor was the moral standard of
the God of the Israelites very much superior
until Amos came. He was a trading God, ready
to offer so much victory for so many sacrifices,
and insistent upon his prerogatives. It was the
high privilege of Amos to proclaim a God who
could not be bought, whose ears were deaf to
pleadings if the cause was unfair, who would
show no discrimination in judgment between the
strong and weak, the rich and poor. It was
a stupendous conception but Amos persuaded
men to accept it, and it has remained a part of
our spiritual heritage.

# HIS METHOD

Years passed and Hosea spoke. His had not been a happy life. His wife deserted him; heartbroken and vengeful he was determined to cast her off forever. Yet his love would not let him do it. He went to her, forgave her, and took her back. Then in his hours of lonely brooding a great thought came to him! If he, a mere man could love so unselfishly one who had broken faith with him, must not God be capable of as great, or greater forgiveness, toward erring human beings? The thought fired his imagination; he stood up before the nation and proclaimed it with burning zeal—a God so strong that he could destroy, yet so tender that he would not!

One God.

A just God.

A good God.

These were the three steps in the development of the greatest of all ideas. Hundreds of generations have died since the days of Moses, of Amos and Hosea. The thought of the world on almost every other subject has changed; but the

conception of God which these three achieved
has remained in control of men's thinking down
to this very hour.

What was there for Jesus to add? Only one
thought, but it was so much more splendid than
all which had gone before that it has altered the
current of history. He invited frail bewildered
humanity to stand upright and look at God face
to face! He called upon men to throw away
fear, disregard the limitations of their mortality,
and claim the Lord of Creation as Father. It
is the basis of all revolt, all democracy. For if
God is the Father of all men, then *all* are his
children and hence the commonest is equally as
precious as the king. No wonder the authorities trembled. They were not fools; they recognized the implications of the teaching. Either
Jesus' life or their power must go. No wonder
that succeeding generations of authorities have
embroidered his Idea and corrupted it, so that
the simplest faith in the world has become a
complex thing of form and ritual, of enforced
observances and "thou shall nots." It was too

dangerous a Power to be allowed to wander the world, unleashed and uncontrolled.

This then was what Jesus wished to send to all creation, through the instrumentality of his eleven men. What were his methods of training? How did he meet prospective believers? How did he deal with objections? By what sort of strategy did he interest and persuade?

He was making the journey back from Jerusalem after his spectacular triumph in cleansing the Temple, when he came to Jacob's Well, and being tired, sat down. His disciples had stopped behind at one of the villages to purchase food, so he was alone. The well furnished the water-supply for the neighboring city of the Samaritans, and after a little time a woman came out to it, carrying her pitcher on her shoulder. Between her people, the Samaritans, and his people, the Jews, there was a feud of centuries. To be touched by even the shadow of a Samaritan was defilement according to the strict code of the Pharisees; to speak to one was a crime. The woman made no concealment of her resentment at finding him there. Almost any remark from his lips would have kindled her anger. She would at least have turned away in scorn; she might have summoned her relatives and driven him off.

An impossible situation, you will admit. How could he meet it? How give his message to one who was forbidden by everything holy to listen? The incident is very revealing: there are times when any word is the wrong word; when only silence can prevail. Jesus knew well this precious secret. As the woman drew closer he made no move to indicate that he was conscious of her approach. His gaze was on the ground. When he spoke it was quietly, musingly, as if to himself:

"If you knew who I am," he said, "you would not need to come out here for water. I would give you living water."

The woman stopped short, her interest challenged in spite of herself; she set down the pitcher and looked at the stranger. It was a burning hot day; the well was far from the city;

she was heated and tired. What did he mean
by such a remark? She started to speak, checked
herself and burst out impulsively, her curiosity
overleaping her caution:

"What are you talking about? Do you mean
to say you are greater than our father Jacob
who gave us this well? Have you some magic
that will save us this long walk in the sun?"

Dramatic, isn't it—a single sentence achieving triumph, arousing interest and creating de-
sire. With sure instinct he followed up his
initial advantage. He began to talk to her in
terms of her own life, her ambitions, her hopes,
knowing so well that each of us is interested first
of all and most of all in himself. When the disciples came up a few minutes later they found an
unbelievable sight—a Samaritan listening with
rapt attention to the teaching of a Jew.

He prepared to go but she would not allow
it. Running back to the city she summoned her
brothers and relatives.

"Come," she cried, "and see a man who told
me all things that ever I did."

They followed her out to the well—these prejudiced, reluctant men and women who, an hour before, would have thought it incredible that they should ever hold conversation with one of their traditional enemies. Suspiciously at first but with steadily ascending interest they listened to his talk. It is said that great leaders are born, not made. The saying is true to this degree, that no man can persuade people to do what he wants them to do, unless he genuinely likes people, and believes that what he wants them to do is to their own advantage. The secret of Jesus' success was an affection for folks which so shone in his eyes and rang in his tones, that even the commonest man in a crowd felt instinctively that here was a friend. . . . The afternoon shadows lengthened while he talked. Other citizens, attracted by the gathering, made their way out to the well and added themselves to the audience. It came time for the evening meal; again he prepared to go. They would not hear of it. He must be their guest, meet their neighbors, tell them more, persuade them further!

"They besought him to abide with them; and he abode there two days."

Some years later a tired pilgrim arrived in the up-to-date and perfectly self-satisfied city of Athens. He arrived on foot because he had no car-fare. His shoes were sadly worn and his clothing unkempt and covered with dust. One would say that these disadvantages were enough to disqualify him for success in a town so smart and critical, but he had other handicaps more fundamental. He was too short and thickset to be impressive; his eyes had a decided squint; altogether he was not at all the kind of man who commands respect before a crowd. That he should come to the most sophisticated center of the ancient world and expect to make an impression was extraordinary. The principal business of the clever gentlemen of that city was standing around the market-place, there to "hear or to tell some new thing." They were the joke-makers and fashion-setters of their era. They originated new ideas; they did not buy them from the provinces. And as for investing in a new religion—they had hundreds of religions, some new, some fairly new, some old, but all entirely unused.

A fine appreciative atmosphere for the foreign visitor named Paul. See him trudging along through the suburbs and up toward the center of the town. Poor little chap; wait until the wise ones catch sight of him; they will certainly make a fine afternoon's sport!

Straight on he marched until he reached Mars Hill, the Broadway and Forty-second Street corner of town. A few of the clever ones gathered about, moved by the same cynical curiosity which would have prompted them to look at a sword swallower or a three legged calf. The critical moment had come. Paul must say something, and no matter what he said, it would be wrong. Suppose he had begun in the usual way: "Good morning, gentlemen, I have something new in the way of a religion which I'd like to explain, if you'll give me just a minute of your time." A boisterous laugh would have ended his talk . . . a new religion . . . what did they care about that?

# HIS METHOD

But Paul knew the psychology of the crowd. "Men of Athens, I congratulate you on having so many fine religions." Nothing in that to which any one could take offense. The sophisticated pressed up a little closer; what was the chap driving at, anyhow? "I've traveled about quite a bit and your assortment is larger and better than I have seen anywhere else. For as I passed up your main street I noticed that you not only have altars erected to all the regular gods and goddesses; you even have one dedicated to the UNKNOWN GOD.

"Let me tell you an interesting coincidence, gentlemen. This God whom you worship without knowing his name, is the very God whom I represent."

Can you see the crowd? Cynical but curious; eager to turn the whole thing into a joke, yet unwilling to miss a chance to hear the latest. Paul stopped short for a moment and voices called out demanding that he go on. It appears later in the narrative that after his talk was over "some mocked, and others said, 'We will hear

thee again of this matter.' " It was not a complete victory such as his Master had achieved at
Jacob's Well; but the audience which had con-
fronted Paul was hostile, and his initial success
so cleverly won, that this story deserves a place
beside the one which we have just related. Together they help us to understand the great
mystery—how a religion, originating in a despised province of a petty country, could so
quickly carry around the world. It conquered
not because there was any *demand* for another
religion but because Jesus knew how, and taught
his followers how, to catch the attention of the
indifferent, and translate a great spiritual conception into terms of practical self-concern.

Surely no one will consider us lacking in
reverence if we say that every one of the "principles of modern salesmanship" on which business men so much pride themselves, are bril-
liantly exemplified in Jesus' talk and work.
The first of these and perhaps the most important is the necessity for "putting yourself in
step with your prospect." A great sales manager used to illustrate it in this way:

"When you want to get aboard a street car which is already in motion, you don't run at it from right angles and try to make the platform in one wild leap," he would say. "If you do, you are likely to find yourself on the floor. No. You run along beside the car, increasing your pace until you are moving just as rapidly as it is moving and in the same direction. Then you step aboard easily, without danger or jolt.

"The minds of busy men are in motion," he would continue. "They are engaged with something very different from the thought you have to present. You can't jump directly at them and expect to make an effective landing. You must put yourself in the other man's place; try to imagine what he is thinking; let your first remark be in line with his thoughts; follow it by another with which you know he will easily agree. Thus, gradually, your two minds reach a point where they can join without conflict. You encourage him to say 'yes' and 'yes' and 'that's right' and 'I've noticed that myself,' until he says the final 'yes' which is your favorable decision."

Jesus taught all this without ever teaching it. Every one of his conversations, every contact between his mind and others, is worthy of the attentive study of any sales manager. Passing along the shores of a lake one day, he saw two of the men whom he wanted as disciples. *Their* minds were in motion; their hands were busy with their nets; their conversation was about conditions in the fishing trade, and the prospects of a good market for the day's catch. To have broken in on such thinking with the offer of employment as preachers of a new religion would have been to confuse them and invite a certain rebuff. What was Jesus' approach?

"Come with me," he said, "and I will make you fishers of men."

Fishers . . . that was a word they could understand . . . fishers of men . . . that was a new idea . . . what was he driving at . . . fishers of men . . . it sounded interesting . . . well, what is it, anyway?

He sat on a hillside overlooking a fertile country. Many of the crowd who gathered

106

around him were farmers, with their wives and sons and daughters. He wanted their interest and attention; it was important to make them understand, at the very outset, that what he had to say was nothing vague or theoretical but of direct and immediate application to their daily lives.

"A sower went forth to sow," he began, "and when he sowed some seeds fell by the wayside and the fowls came and devoured them up. . . ." Were they interested . . . *were* they? Every man of them had gone through that experience . . . the thievish crows . . . many a good day's work *they* had spoiled. . . . So this Teacher knew something about the troubles that farmers had to put up with, did he? Fair enough . . . let's hear what he has to say. . . .

It would be easy to multiply examples, taking each of his parables and pointing out the keen knowledge of human motives on which it is based. In a later chapter we shall have something more to say of these parables—the most powerful advertisements of all time. For our present purpose the examples already given are enough. They show how instantly he won his audiences. With his very first sentence he put himself in step with them; it was invariably a thought in line with their own thinking, easy for even the dullest to understand, and shrewdly calculated to awaken an appetite for more.

Every salesman knows the value of being able to sense an objection and meet it before it is advanced. Jesus knew that far better. He went one night to dine with a prominent Pharisee. His presence in any house attracted strangers who found it easy under the less rigid conventions of those days, to make their way into the room, where they could watch him and listen. Thus, while the Pharisee's dinner was in progress, a certain woman of unfortunate experience crept into the room and kneeling down by Jesus began to bathe his feet with precious ointment and wipe them with her hair. Jesus knew what that outburst of unselfishness meant to an over-burdened spirit, and accepted the tribute with gracious dignity, even though its emotional warmth must have been embarrassing. But all the time he was perfectly well aware of the thoughts that were passing through the self-satisfied mind of his host.

"Ah," said that cynical gentleman to himself, "if he were a prophet he would have known that this woman is a sinner, and would have refused to let her touch him."

He might have been tempted to put his thought into words, but he never had a chance. Quick as a flash Jesus turned on him:

"Simon, I have somewhat to say to thee."

"Teacher, say on." It was a half concealed sneer.

"There was a man who had two debtors," said Jesus. "One owed him five hundred shillings and the other fifty. Neither could pay and he forgave them both. Which of them, do you think, will love him most?"

Simon sensed a trap, and moved cautiously.

"I imagine the one who owed him the most," said he, and wondered what was coming next.

"Right," said Jesus. "Simon, seest thou this woman?"

Simon nodded. He began to wish the conversation had not started.

"When I came into your house, you gave me no water for my feet," Jesus continued with that extraordinary frankness which cut straight to the heart of things. "But she has washed my feet with her tears and dried them with her hair. You gave me no kiss, but she has not ceased to kiss my feet. You poured none of your expensive oil on my head, but she has taken her precious ointment, which she could ill-afford, and anointed me."

Simon squirmed in his seat. It was not comfortable to be reminded before a crowd of his delinquencies as a host. He had invited this "interesting" ex-carpenter because it was quite the fad to invite him. But the whole atmosphere had been one of condescension—the unspoken intimation was, "Here's a good dinner; now go on and amuse us with your ideas." There had been none of the niceties; the rich are so well accustomed to being inconsiderate!

The dining-room was silent; every eye was

turned upon the Teacher; the poor woman still knelt at his feet, embarrassed that her action should have caused so much comment, wondering if the incident was to end in a rebuke. Jesus did not look down at her; he was not yet through with Simon.

"She is like the debtor who owed the five hundred shillings," he said. "Her sins which are many are forgiven, for she loved much. To whom little is forgiven, the same loves little." And then with a glance of infinite tenderness:

"Thy sins are forgiven," he said to her simply. "Thy faith has saved thee; go in peace."

It is easy to imagine that the conversation rather dragged during the remainder of the meal. Even very supercilious and self-assured gentlemen hesitated to expose themselves to the thrusts of a mind which could anticipate criticisms before they were uttered, and deal with them so crisply.

On other occasions he won his case with a single question—one of the best weapons in the whole armory of persuasion and all too infrequently employed. How often a blundering advocate allows himself to be dragged into futile argument, when by throwing the burden back on to his opponent's shoulders he could attain an easy mastery. Jesus seldom argued. The record of his questions is a fruitful study for all of us who, in our every-day affairs, must deal with other minds. Let us recall two of those questions.

The Pharisees set a trap for him. One Sabbath day they hunted up a man with a withered hand and deposited him in the Temple where Jesus would be sure to pass. Then they waited. If Jesus healed him, it would be a breach of the Code, which forbade any activity on the Sabbath. They would have that to recall when the crisis came. Jesus sensed the test and met it without hesitation.

"Stand forth," he said to the poor chap.

The bigoted formalists pushed in close. This was their moment. They had dug the pit cleverly and now he was about to fall in. The soft light went out of Jesus' eyes, the muscles of his jaw grew tense, he looked "round on them with anger," as he demanded:

"Is it lawful on the Sabbath day to do good or to do harm? To save a life or to kill?"

He waited for an answer but none came. What could they say? If they replied that the law forbade a good deed, their answer would be repeated all over town. The crowd of common folks who followed him were his friends, not theirs—only too glad to spread a story which would cast discredit on the proud defenders of the law. The Pharisees had sense enough to recognize that fact, at least. They "held their peace," and sullenly slipped away.

On another day it was his own disciples who learned how he could compress a whole philosophy into a well-directed interrogation. They were by no means free from the frailties of ordinary human nature. They fussed about little things—arguing among themselves as to who should have preeminence; wondering how their bills were to be met, and just where the whole enterprise was coming out.

He brought them up short with a question.

"Which of you by being anxious can add a single day to his life?" he demanded. "And if you can't do this simple thing, why worry about the rest? Consider the ravens; they don't sow or reap; they have no store-houses or barns, and yet God takes care of them. Don't you suppose that you are of more value in his sight than a flock of birds?"

How trivial seemed their concern and controversy after a question like that!

In all the three years of his public work there was not one moment when he failed to be complete master of the situation. He was accessible to anybody—in the market-place, in the temple and on the main streets—fair game for the keen and clever. It became quite a recognized sport to match wits with him. Pharisees tried it; Scribes tried it; "a certain lawyer" tried it. Always they came off second best. At length the very chiefs of the priests came one afternoon. Lesser antagonists had gone down; now the leaders themselves would take the matter in hand. They would demolish this presumptuous upstart; by the splendor of their presence and their offices, they would awe him into line.

"By what authority do you do these things," they demanded bruskly, "and who gave you this authority?"

If they expected him to yield an inch they received the surprise of their lives. His retort was instantaneous.

"I'll ask you a question," he exclaimed, "and if you answer it, then I'll tell you by what authority I work. Answer me now, what about John; was his work in baptizing inspired by Heaven or by men?"

They caught their breath. Their heads came together; excited and disturbing whispers were exchanged. What should they say? If we answer that John had come from Heaven, he will say, "Well, why then didn't you believe him?" If we say, that he came from men, this crowd of fools will tear us to pieces, because every last one of them believes that John was a prophet. What shall we do? Better tell him we don't know; better get out of here as quickly as we can.

"We don't know," they muttered.

"All right," said Jesus serenely. "You don't answer my question. Neither will I answer yours."

It was a perfect triumph. Amid the jeers of the delighted crowd they gathered up their fine robes and went away.

You would think as you read the narratives that the wise ones would have been wise enough to let him alone. Even a child having burned its fingers once, knows enough to avoid the fire. But their jealousy and anger drove them back again and again; and every time he was too much for them. In the very last week the "Pharisees and Herodians" gathered together a picked delegation of sharp wits and sent them with what looked like an absolutely fool-proof bomb. They started in with flattery; after all he was a simple fellow from the provinces—a few kind words and his head would be turned. Then they would catch him off his guard.

"Teacher, we know that you speak the truth."

they said, "and that you don't care anything about the authority or office which a man holds. You treat them all alike, and speak your mind bluntly because you get your thoughts direct from God.

"Now, tell us, is it lawful to give tribute unto Cæsar or not?"

Very clever, gentlemen, very clever indeed. If he answers that it *isn't* lawful, you will have the record of his reply in Herod's hands in an hour; and instantly he will be under arrest for propagating rebellion against the Roman power; if he answers that it *is* lawful, he will lose his popular following. Because the people hate the Romans, and dodge the taxes at every turn . . . very, very clever.

He looked at them with frank contempt, as if to say, "Do you really think I am quite as simple as all that?"

"Somebody lend me a coin," he exclaimed. An eager listener dug into his pocket and produced it. Jesus held it up where all could see.

"Whose picture is that?" he demanded. "Whose name?"

They began to be uneasy. The shrewdest suspected that the path was leading toward the precipice, yet there was no escape. They must answer. "Cæsar's," they replied.

"Very good," said he ironically. "Render unto Cæsar the things that are Cæsar's and unto God the things that are God's."

Another repulse for the best legal talent in the city . . . another good laugh for the crowd . . . another story to tell in the taverns, in the Temple court, in the market-place . . . wherever the common folks crowded together. . . . Says the narrative describing the defeated questioners: "they marveled greatly at him." . . . and in another place . . . "and no man after that durst ask him any question." Every objection had been turned back upon the objectors; every trap had sprung upon the fingers of those who set it. No argument was left for them except the final one which is always a confession of failure. They had the brute force on their side. They could not stand against his thinking but they could, and did, nail him on the cross.

Not in time, however. Not until his work was
finished. Not until he had trained and equipped
a force which would carry on with double power
because of the very fact of his death. . . . Every
year in our country there are thousands of conventions—political, charitable, business. Most
of them are a waste. They are conducted on
the false assumption that over-selling and ex-
aggeration are potent forces—that the energies
of men respond most powerfully to promises of
easy victory and soft rewards. The great leaders
of the world have known better.

Gideon, for example. When he called for vol-
unteers to fight the Midianites, thirty-two thousand responded. Gideon looked them over crit-
ically. He knew the conflicting motives that
had brought them there—some from mere love
of adventure; some because they were afraid to
be taunted with cowardice; some for plunder;
some to get away from their wives. He determined to weed them out at once:

"Whosoever is fearful and afraid, let him go
home to-night," he proclaimed.

The next morning twenty-two thousand had vanished. Only ten thousand remained.

Still Gideon was unsatisfied. He hit upon a stratagem. Down the hillside and across a little brook he led the whole band. It was a hot morning; the men were thirsty and tired; and Gideon, standing on the bank and watching, had a shrewd idea that character would show itself under the strain. Sure enough, of the ten thousand, a vast majority knelt down and pushed their faces into the cool clear water, taking long refreshing draughts. But a few were too eager. They caught up the water in their hands, dashed it into their faces, and hurried across to the other bank, restless to be on!

Only a handful; only three hundred. But Gideon kept them and sent the rest home. Better three hundred who could not be held back from the battle than ten thousand who were merely half-heartedly ready to go.

With the three hundred he won.

That higher type of leadership which calls forth men's greatest energies by the promise of

obstacles rather than the picture of rewards—
that was the leadership of Jesus. By it he tempered the soft metal of his disciples' nature into keen hard steel. The final conference with which he prepared them for their work is thrilling in its majestic appeal to courage. Listen to the calm recital of the deprivations and dangers:

Get you no gold, nor silver, nor brass in your purses.

No wallet for your journey; neither two coats, nor shoes nor staff.

Behold I send you forth as sheep in the midst of wolves.

Beware of men: for they will deliver you up to councils and in their synagogues they will scourge you; yea and before governors and kings shall ye be brought for my sake.

He that loveth father or mother more than me is not worthy of me: and he that loveth son or daughter more than me is not worthy of me. And he that doth not take his cross and follow after me is not worthy of me.

He that findeth his life shall lose it; and he that loseth his life for my sake shall find it.

Watch the faces and the figures. See the shoulders straighten, the muscles of the lips grow hard. There is power in those faces that will not be withstood—power born of the most transforming appeal which ever fell on human ears. The voice of the speaker was stilled at the cross, but the power carried on. It withstood prisons and scourging; ship-wreck and weariness; public condemnation and the loss of personal friends; chains, and the roar of lions and the flames. James was the first to die. Herod Agrippa killed him. His brother John, imprisoned for years on the stony island of Patmos, suffered martyrdom amidst frightful torture. Andrew died on a cross whose pattern bears his name to this day. Simon Peter insisted that he be crucified head downward, deeming himself unworthy to suffer in the manner of his Lord. Nero stilled the voice of Paul by beheading him; but the spirit of Paul which had proclaimed that "we are in all things more than conquerors," began at that moment to have its larger influence.

Just a few brief years and every member of

the original organization was gone, but the "blood of the martyrs was the seed of the church." The Master's training had done its work.

The great Idea prevailed.

# CHAPTER V

## His Advertisements

He was, as we say, "many sided," and every man sees the side of his nature which appeals most to himself.

The doctor thinks of the great physician whose touch never failed, who by some mystery preceded modern science in its still imperfect knowledge of the relation of the spirit to health. The preacher studies the Sermon on the Mount and marvels that truths so profound should be expressed in words so clear and simple. The agitator remembers only that he denounced the rich; and the communist that his disciples carried a common purse. Lawyers have written in praise of his pleading at his trial; and the literary critics of every age have cheerfully acknowledged his mastery.

I am not a doctor, or lawyer or critic but an

advertising man. As a profession advertising
is young; as a force it is as old as the world. The
first four words ever uttered, "Let there be
light," constitute its charter. All Nature is
vibrant with its impulse. The brilliant plumage
of the bird is color advertising addressed to the
emotions of its mate. Plants deck themselves
with blossoms, not for beauty only, but to at-
tract the patronage of the bee and so by spread-
ing pollen on its wings, to insure the perpetua-
tion of their kind.

> The spacious firmament on high,
> And all the blue ethereal sky,
> And spangled Heavens a shining frame,
> Their great Original *proclaim*.

It has been remarked that "no astronomer can
be an atheist," which is only another way of saying that no man can look up at the first and
greatest electric sign—the evening stars—and
refuse to believe its message: "There is a Cause:
A God." I propose in this chapter to speak of
the advertisements of Jesus which have survived

for twenty centuries and are still the most potent influence in the world.

Let us begin by asking why he was so successful in mastering public attention and why, in contrast, his churches are less so? The answer is twofold. In the first place he recognized the basic principle that all good advertising is news. He was never trite or commonplace; he had no routine. If there had been newspapers in those days, no city editor could have said, "No need to visit him to-day; he will be doing just what he did last Sunday." Reporters would have followed him every single hour, for it was impossible to predict what he would say or do; every action and word were news.

Take one single day as an example. The four gospel narratives are not chronological. They are personal records written after his death, not diaries in which entries were made every night. Thus we can not say of most of the incidents: "This happened on such and such a day." The four stories repeat and conflict and overlap. In one place, however—the ninth chapter of Matthew—we have a detailed account of a single day's work. One of the events was the calling of Matthew himself to discipleship; hence we have every reason to suppose that the writer's memory of this particular day must have been more than usually reliable. Let us look at the twenty-four hours' schedule; see how it bristles with front-page news.

The activity begins at sunrise. Jesus was an early riser; he knew that the simplest way to live *more* than an average life is to add an hour to the fresh end of the day. At sunrise, therefore, we discover a little boat pushing out from the shore of the lake. It makes its steady way across and deposits Jesus and his disciples in Capernaum, his favorite city. He proceeds at once to the house of a friend, but not without being discovered. The report spreads instantly that he is in town, and before he can finish breakfast a crowd has collected outside the gate—a poor palsied chap among them.

The day's work is at hand.

Having slept soundly in the open air he meets

the call with quiet nerves. The smile that carried confidence into even the most hopeless heart spreads over his features; he stoops down toward the sufferer.

"Be of good cheer, my son," he cries, "your sins are all forgiven."

Sins forgiven! Indeed! The respectable members of the audience draw back with sharp disapproval. "What a blasphemous phrase," they exclaim. "Who authorized him to exercise the functions of God? What right has he to decide whose sins shall be forgiven?"

Jesus sensed rather than heard their protest. He never courted controversy but he never dodged it; and much of his fame arose out of the reports of his verbal victories. Men have been elected to office—even such high office as the Presidency—by being so good-natured that they never made an enemy. But the leaders who are remembered are those who had plenty of critics and dealt with them vigorously.

"What's the objection?" he exclaimed, turning on the dissenters. "Why do you stand there and criticize? Is it easier to say, "Thy sins be forgiven thee,' or to say, 'Arise, take up thy bed and walk?' The results are the same." Bending over the sick man again he said: "Arise, take up thy bed and go unto thine house."

The man stirred and was amazed to find that his muscles responded. Slowly, doubtingly he struggled to his feet, and with one great shout of happiness started off, surrounded by his jubilant friends. The critics had received their answer, but they refused to give up. For an hour or more they persisted in angry argument, until the meeting ended in a tumult.

Can you imagine the next day's issue of the *Capernaum News,* if there had been one?

PALSIED MAN HEALED

JESUS OF NAZARETH CLAIMS RIGHT TO

FORGIVE SINS

PROMINENT SCRIBES OBJECT

"BLASPHEMOUS," SAYS LEADING CITIZEN.

"BUT ANYWAY I CAN WALK," HEALED MAN

RETORTS.

129

Front page story number one and the day is still young.

One of those who had been attracted by the excitement was a tax-collector named Matthew. Being a man of business he could not stay through the argument, but slipped away early and was hard at work when Jesus passed by a few minutes before noon.

"Matthew, I want you," said Jesus.

That was all. No argument; no offer of inducements; no promise of rewards. Merely "I want you;" and the prosperous tax-collector closed his office, made a feast for the brilliant young teacher and forthwith announced himself a disciple.

\* \* \*

PROMINENT TAX COLLECTOR JOINS

NAZARETH FORCES

MATTHEW ABANDONS BUSINESS TO PROMOTE

NEW CULT

\* \* \*

GIVES LARGE LUNCHEON

Front page story number two.

The luncheon itself furnished the third sensation. It was not at all the kind of affair which a religious teacher would be expected to approve. Decidedly it was good-natured and noisy.

No theological test was applied in limiting the invitation. No one stood at the entrance to demand: "What is your belief regarding the birth of Jesus?" Or, "Have you or have you not been baptized?" The doors were flung wide, and, along with the disciples and the respectable folks, a swarm of publicans and sinners trooped in.

"Outrageous," grumbled the worthy folk. "Surely if this teacher had any moral standards he never would eat with such rabble."

They were shocked; but he was not. That he had condemned himself according to their formula worried him not a whit. His liking for folks overran all social boundaries; he just could not seem to remember that some people are nice people, proper people, and some are not.

"Come, come," he exclaimed to the Pharisees, "won't you ever get over nagging at me because I eat with these outsiders? Who needs the doctor most—they that are well or they that are sick?

"And here's another thing to think about," he added. "You lay so much stress on forms and creeds and occasions—do you suppose God cares about all that? What do you think he meant when he said: 'I will have mercy and not sacrifice?' Take that home and puzzle over it."

DEFENDS PUBLICANS AND SINNERS

\* \* \*

JESUS OF NAZARETH WELCOMES THEM AT LUNCH

\* \* \*

REBUKES PROMINENT PHARISEES

\* \* \*

"CREEDS UNIMPORTANT," HE SAYS. "GOD WANTS
MERCY NOT SACRIFICE."

A fourth big story. You may be sure it was carried into hundreds of homes during the next few weeks, and formed the basis for many a long evening's discussion.

As the meal drew to its close there came a dramatic interruption—a ruler of the city made his way slowly to the head of the table and stood silent, bowed by the terrible weight of his grief. That morning he had sat at his daughter's bedside, clasping her frail white hand in his, watching the flutter of the pulse, trying by the force of his longing to hold that little life back from the precipice. And at last the doctors had told him that it was useless any more to hope. So he had come, this ruler, to the strange young man whose deeds of healing were the sensation of the day.

Was it too late? The ruler had thought so when he entered the door; but as he stood in that splendid presence a new thrilling conviction gripped him:

"Master, my daughter is even now dead," he exclaimed, "but come and lay your hand on her and she will live."

Jesus rose from his seat, drawn by that splendid outburst of faith and without hesitation or questioning he started for the door. All his life he seemed to feel that there was no limit at all to what he could do, if only those who beseeched him believed enough. Grasping the ruler's arm he led the way up the street, his disciples and the motley crowd hurrying along behind.

They had several blocks to travel, and before their journey was completed another interruption occurred.

A woman who had been sick for twelve years edged through the crowd, eluded the sharp eyes of the disciples and touched the hem of his garment. "For she said within herself, if I may but touch his garment, I shall be whole." . . . What an idea. . . . What a Personality his must have been to provoke such ideas. . . . "My daughter is dead, but lay your hands on her and she will live." . . . "I've been sick for twelve years; the doctors can do nothing, but if I only touch his coat I'll be all right." . . . How can the artists possibly have imagined that a sad-faced weakling could ever inspire such amazing ideas as these!

The woman won her victory. By that touch, by his smile, by the few words he spoke, her faith rose triumphant over disease. She "was made whole from that hour."

Again he moved forward, the crowd pressing hard. The ruler's residence was now in plain sight. The paid mourners, hired by the hour, were busy about the doorway; they increased their activities as their employer came in sight —hideous wails and the dull sounding of cymbals—a horrible pretense of grief. Quickening his stride Jesus was in the midst of them.

"Give place," he cried with a commanding gesture. "The maid is not dead but sleepeth."

They laughed him to scorn. Brushing them aside he strode into the house and took the little girl by the hand. The crowd looked on dumfounded, for at the magic of his touch she opened her eyes, and sat up.

Front page stories five and six. A woman sick twelve years, and healed! A child whom the doctors had abandoned for dead, sits up and smiles! No wonder a thousand tongues were busy that night advertising his name and work. "The fame thereof went abroad into all that land," says the narrative. Nothing could keep it from going abroad. It was irresistible news!

He was advertised by his service, not by his sermons; this is the second noteworthy fact. No-where in the Gospels do you find it announced that:

Jesus of Nazareth Will Denounce
The Scribes and Pharisees in the
Central Synagogue
To-night at Eight O'Clock
Special Music

His preaching was almost incidental. On only one occasion did he deliver a long discourse, and that was probably interrupted often by questions and debates. He did not come to establish a theology but to lead a life. Living more healthfully than any of his contemporaries he spread health wherever he went. Thinking

136

more daringly, more divinely, he expressed himself in thoughts of surpassing beauty, as naturally as a plant bursts into bloom. His sermons, if they may be called sermons, were chiefly explanatory of his service. He healed a lame man, gave sight to a blind man, fed the hungry, cheered the poor; and by these works he was advertised much more than by his words.

The church, which covets advertising and receives little, is much more fruitful in such good works than the man on the street suspects. Most of our colleges were founded under its inspiration; most of our hospitals grew out of, and are supported by, its membership; the ideals that animate all civic enterprises are its ideals; and its members furnish to such movements the most dependable support. More than this, the day by day life of any genuine pastor is a constant succession of healings and helpings, as any one who has been privileged to grow up in a minister's family very well knows. The door-bell rings at breakfast-time; it rings at dinner-time; it rings late at night—and every ring means that some one has come to cast his burden upon the parsonage. A man comes blinded by his greed or hatred or fear—he opens his heart to the pastor, and goes away having received his sight. A parent whose child is dead in selfishness, comes leading the child by the hand. And sometimes the preacher is able to touch the withered veins of conscience, and life becomes normal and wholesome again. A man out of work, whose family is hungry, knocks timidly at the parsonage door. And somehow, from the parson's few loaves and fishes, the other family is fed.

*These* are Jesus' works, done in Jesus' name. If he were to live again, in these modern days, he would find a way to make them known—to be advertised by his service, not merely by his sermons. One thing is certain: he would not neglect the market-place. Few of his sermons were delivered in synagogues. For the most part he was in the crowded places, the Temple Court, the city squares, the centers where goods were bought and sold. I emphasized this fact once to a group of preachers.

"You mean that we ought to do street preaching," one of them exclaimed.

But street preaching is not at all analogous to what Jesus did. The cities in which he worked were both small and leisurely; the market was a gathering place where everybody came at some time—the transfer place for all merchandise and for ideas. Where will you find such a market-place in modern days? A corner of Fifth Avenue? A block on Broadway? Only a tiny fraction of the city's people pass any given point in the down-town district on any given day. A man might stand and preach for years at Fifth Avenue and Thirtieth Street, and only one in a hundred thousand would ever know that he lived.

No; the present day market-place is the newspaper and the magazine. Printed columns are the modern thoroughfares; published advertisements are the cross-roads where the sellers and the buyers meet. Any issue of a national magazine is a world's fair, a bazaar filled with the products of the world's work. Clothes and clocks and candle-sticks; soup and soap and cigarettes; lingerie and limousines—the best of all of them are there, proclaimed by their makers in persuasive tones. That every other voice should be raised in such great market-places, and the voice of Jesus of Nazareth be still—this is a vital omission which he would find a way to correct. He would be a national advertiser to-day, I am sure, as he was the great advertiser of his own day. To the minds of those who hurry through the bristling pages, he too would send his call:

What shall it profit a man if he shall gain the whole world and lose his own soul; or what shall a man give in exchange for his soul?

This would be his challenge in every newspaper and magazine; and with it would be coupled an invitation to share in the joyous enterprise of his work.

A very successful publisher has a rule that no photograph shall ever be printed in his newspapers unless it contains human beings. You and I are interested most of all in ourselves; next to that we are interested *in other people.* What do they look like? How old are they? What have they done and said? With unerring instinct Jesus recognized and used this trait in human nature. One of the most revealing of all verses to those who would understand the secret of his power is this: "All these things spake Jesus unto the multitude *in parables;* and without a parable spake he not unto them." A parable is a story. He told them stories, stories about people, and let the stories carry his message. He might have adopted very different methods—many teachers and would-be leaders do. He might have dealt in generalities, saying:

"When you are going about your business, be as kind as you can. Be thoughtful of the other travelers on the highways of life. Take time to look for those who have fared less fortunately; lend them a helping hand whenever you can."

I say he *might* have uttered such generalities. But if he had, do you suppose that they would ever have been remembered? Would the disciples have recorded them? Would our age ever have heard his name? He was far wiser in the laws and habits of the human mind. Instead of the commonplace phrases written above, he painted this striking picture:

A certain man went down from Jerusalem to Jericho and fell among thieves.

There's your illustration and your head-line! If you had lived near Jerusalem or Jericho; if you often had occasion to use that very road, wouldn't you want to know what happened to that unfortunate traveler?

"They stripped off his raiment," the parable continues, "and wounded him, and departed, leaving him half dead." Pretty soon a priest came by and seeing the victim said to himself: "That's a shameful thing, the police ought to do something about these outrages." But he crossed over carefully and passed by on the other side. A certain respectable Levite also appeared. "His own fault," he sniffed, "ought to be more careful." And he too passed by. Then a third traveler drew near, and stopped—and the whole world knows what happened. . . . Generalities would have been soon forgotten. But the story that had its roots in every-day human experience and need, lives and will live forever. It condenses the philosophy of Christianity into a half dozen unforgetable paragraphs. The parable of the Good Samaritan is the greatest advertisement of all time.

Take any one of the parables, no matter which —you will find that it exemplifies all the principles on which advertising text books are written. Always a picture in the very first sentence; crisp, graphic language and a message so clear that even the dullest can not escape it.

### Ten Virgins Went Forth To Meet
### A Bridegroom

A striking picture and a striking head-line. The story which follows has not a single wasted word:

Five of the Virgins were wise, and five were foolish.

They that were foolish took their lamps, and took no oil with them:

But the wise took oil in their vessels with their lamps.

While the bridegroom tarried, they all slumbered and slept.

And at midnight there was a cry made, Behold the bridegroom cometh; go ye out to meet him.

Then all those Virgins arose, and trimmed their lamps.

And the foolish said unto the wise, "Give us of your oil for our lamps have gone out."

But the wise answered, saying, "Not so; lest there be not enough for us and you; but go ye rather to them that sell, and buy for yourselves."

And while they went to buy, the bridegroom came; and they that were ready went in with him to the marriage; and the door was shut.

Afterward came also the other Virgins, saying, "Lord, Lord, open to me."

But he answered and said, "Verily, I say unto you, I know you not . . . "

Watch, therefore, for ye know neither the day nor the hour wherein the Son of man cometh.

Illustrate that with a drawing by a distinguished artist; set it up according to the best modern typography; bury it in a magazine with a hundred other pages—will it not stand out? Will it not grip the attention of even the most casual, and *make* itself read?

Here is another one:

## What Happened To The One Lost Sheep

What man of you, having a hundred sheep, if he lose one of them, doth not leave the ninety and nine in the wilderness, and go after that which is lost, until he find it?

And when he hath found it, he layeth it on his shoulders rejoicing.

And when he cometh home, he calleth his friends and neighbors, saying unto them, "Rejoice with me; for I have found my sheep which was lost." . . .

I say unto you, that likewise joy shall be in heaven over one sinner that repenteth, more than over ninety and nine just persons which need no repentance. . . . "

If you were given the task of advertising to the world that God cares enormously for one human life—no matter how wayward and wrong the life may be—how could you phrase a message more memorable than that? Yet how simple; how sincere; how splendidly crisp and direct. Benjamin Franklin in his autobiography—that first great American "success story"—tells the process through which he went in acquiring an effective style. He would read a passage from some great master of English, then lay the book aside and attempt to reproduce the thought in his own words. Comparing his version with the original, he discovered wherein he had obscured the thought, or wasted words, or failed in driving straight to the point. Every advertising man ought to study the parables of Jesus in the same fashion, schooling himself in their language and learning these four big elements of their power.

1. First of all they are marvelously condensed, as all good advertising must be. Charles A. Dana, once issued an assignment to a new reporter on the *New York Sun*, directing him to confine his article to a column. The reporter protested that the story was too big to be compressed into so small a space.

"Get a copy of the Bible and read the first

chapter of Genesis," said Dana. "You'll be surprised to find that the whole story of the creation of the world can be told in 600 words."

It is an axiom in many magazine offices that the introduction to almost any article can be cut by the editor without sacrificing anything of real value. Even experienced writers almost invariably *write* something before they begin to *say* anything. Advertising writers are compelled to greater condensation, but they too are guilty of much waste in words. How often you must read and read before you discover just what it is that the advertiser wants you to do. Jesus had no introductions. A single sentence grips your attention; three or four more tell the story; one or two more and the application is driven home. When he wanted a new disciple he said simply "Follow me." When he sought to explain the deepest philosophic mystery—the personality and character of God—he said, "A king made a banquet and invited many guests. God is that king and you are the guests; the Kingdom of Heaven is happiness—a banquet to be enjoyed."

Two men spoke on the battleground of Gettysburg sixty years ago. The first delivered an oration of more than two hours in length; not one person in ten who reads this page can even recall his name; certainly not one in a hundred can quote a single sentence from that "masterly effort." The second speaker uttered two hundred and fifty words, and those words, Lincoln's Gettysburg Address, are a part of the mental endowment of almost every American.

Many noble prayers have been sent up to the Throne of Grace—long impressive utterances. The prayer which Jesus taught his disciples consists of sixty-eight words, and can be written on the back of a post-card. Many poems and essays have been penned by writers who hoped that they were making a permanent place for themselves in literature; but the greatest poem ever written consists of one hundred and eighty-eight words. It is the Twenty-Third Psalm.

Jesus hated prosy dullness. He praised the Centurion who was anxious not to waste his time; the only prayer which he publicly commended was uttered by a poor publican who merely cried out, "God, be merciful to me a sinner." A seven word prayer, Jesus called it a good one. A sixty-eight word prayer, he said, contained all that men needed to say or God to hear. What would be his verdict on most of our prayers and our speeches and our advertisements?

2. His language was marvelously simple—a second great essential. There is hardly a sentence in his teaching which a child can not understand. His illustrations were all drawn from the commonest experiences of life; "a sower went forth to sow"; "a certain man had two sons"; "a man built his house on the sands"; "the kingdom of heaven is like a grain of mustard seed." The absence of adjectives is striking. Henry Ward Beecher said once that "to a large extent adjectives are like leaves on a switch; they may make it look pretty, as a branch, but they prevent it striking tinglingly when you use it.

"I recollect a case in which my father at a public meeting was appointed to draw up an article," Beecher continued. "He had written one sentence: 'It is wrong.' Some one in the meeting got up and moved in his enthusiasm that this be corrected, and that the sentence read: 'It is exceedingly wrong.' My father got up and said, in his mild way, 'When I was writing out this resolution in its original shape that was the way I wrote it, but to make it stronger, I took out the "exceedingly." ' "

Jesus used few qualifying words and no long ones. We referred a minute ago to those three literary masterpieces, The Lord's Prayer, The Twenty-Third Psalm, The Gettysburg Address. Recall their phraseology:

Our Father which art in Heaven, hallowed be thy name

* * *

The Lord is my shepherd; I shall not want

* * *

Four score and seven years ago

* * *

Not a single three-syllable word; hardly any two-syllable words. All the greatest things in human life are one-syllable things—love, joy, hope, home, child, wife, trust, faith, God—and the great advertisements generally speaking, are those in which the most small words are found.

3. Sincerity glistened like sunshine through every sentence he uttered; sincerity is the third essential. Many wealthy men have purchased newspapers with the idea of advancing their personal fortunes, or bringing about some political action in which they have a private interest. Such newspapers almost invariably fail. No matter how much money is spent on them, no matter how zealously the secret of their ownership is guarded, the readers are conscious that something is wrong. They feel that the voice of the editor is not his own. The public has a sixth sense for detecting insincerity; they know instinctively when words ring true.

It was the way Jesus looked at men, and the life he led among them that gave his words transforming power. What he was and what he said were one and the same thing. Nobody could stand at his side for even a minute without being persuaded that here was a man who loved people and considered even the humblest of them worthy of the best he had to give. There is no superstition more deadening to a writer than the idea that he can "write down" to his readers. No man was ever big enough to build an enduring success on the basis of insincerity; but many comparatively small men, like Peter the Hermit or Billy Sunday, fired with conviction, have been able to create and sustain a very considerable influence.

Jesus was notably tolerant of almost all kinds of sinners. He liked the companionship of the rough and ready folk who were entirely outside the churches; he was tender toward unfortunate women; he had a special fondness for James and John whose ungovernable tempers had given them the title of "Sons of Thunder"; he forgave the weakness of Peter who denied him; and was not resentful at the unbelief of his near relatives and his native town. But for one sin he had no mercy. He denounced the *insincerity* of the Pharisees in phrases which sting like the lash of a whip. They thought they had a first mortgage on the Kingdom of Heaven, and he told them scornfully that only those who become like little children have any chance of entering in.

Little children know no pretense. They are startlingly frank. They look at the world through clear eyes and say only what they think. No writer, no orator, no salesman, exercises any large dominion in the world unless he can humble himself and partake of their nature.

"Though I speak with the tongues of men and of angels and have not love, I am become as sounding brass or a tinkling cymbal," wrote Saint Paul.

Much brass has been sounded and many cymbals tinkled in the name of advertising; but the advertisements which persuade people to act are written by men who have an abiding respect for the intelligence of their readers, and a deep sincerity regarding the merits of the goods they have to sell.

**4.** Finally he knew the necessity for repetition and practised it. One of the sons of President Garfield was traveling with him through Ohio, when the President was addressing county fairs. At the close of the day he asked his boy what he thought of his speeches. The boy was embarrassed by the question:

"Why . . . why they were fine, dad," he stammered, "but I felt awfully uncomfortable part of the time. You repeated yourself so often; once you said the very same thing in different words four times over."

Garfield slapped the boy's shoulder with a hearty laugh.

"So you thought your old dad was running out of ideas, did you?" he cried. "Well, I don't blame you; but there's a method in his madness. To-morrow when I reach that passage in my talk, you watch the audience. The first time I make the point, you'll see by their faces that a few folks near the platform get it. But further back there will be noise and commotion; people will be turning their heads to find out who has just driven up, or what sort of a hat Mrs. Jones has on, and they won't hear me at all. When I repeat it the first time a few faces in the middle of the crowd will show a response; on the third go, I'll make still more converts, and on the fourth trial they'll all have a notion of what I am talking about. But it takes four shots to land them all; experience with all sorts of audiences has made me sure of that."

It has been said that "reputation is repetition." No important truth can be impressed upon the minds of any large number of people by being said only once. The thoughts which Jesus had to give the world were revolutionary, but they were few in number. "God is your father," he said, "caring more for the welfare of every one of you than any human father can possibly care for his children. His Kingdom is happiness! his rule is love." This is what he had to teach, but he knew the necessity of driving it home from every possible angle. So in one of his stories God is the shepherd searching the wilds for one wandering sheep; in another, the

Father welcoming home a prodigal boy; in another a King who forgives his debtors large amounts and expects them to be forgiving in turn—*many* stories, *many* advertisements, but the same big Idea.

Because the advertisements were unforgettable, the Idea lived, and is to-day the one most powerful influence on human action and thought. To be sure the work of the advertisements is far from complete. The Idea that God is the Father of *all* men—not merely of a specially selected few—has still to penetrate some creeds, and to establish its dominance in society. More or less unconsciously a lot of us share the feeling of the French nobleman in St. Simon's immortal story who was sure that God would "think twice before damning a person of his quality." Said the Duchess of Buckingham to the Countess of Huntingdon, in a delicious letter:

I thank your Ladyship for the information concerning the Methodist preachers; their doctrines are most repulsive and strongly tinctured with impertinence and disrespect toward their superiors. . . . It is monstrous to be told you have a heart as sinful as the common wretches that crawl on the earth. This is highly offensive and insulting, and I cannot but wonder that your Ladyship should relish any sentiments so much at variance with high rank and good breeding.

In spite of all the Duchesses of Buckingham, however, the Great Advertisements continue to make progress. Monarchies are succeeded by democracies, building their governments on the firm foundation that men are free and equally entitled to a chance at the good things of life. The privileged protest and the agitator denounces, but unmistakably the world is becoming every day a fairer, juster and happier living place for the great majority of its inhabitants.

And whoever feels an impulse to make his own life count in this grand process of human betterment, can have no surer guide for his activities than the advertisements of Jesus. Let him learn their lesson, that if you would teach people you first must capture their interest with news; that your service rather than your sermons must be your claim upon their attention; that what you say must be simple, and brief, and above all *sincere*—the unmistakable voice of true regard and affection.

"Ye," said he, "are my *friends.*"

# CHAPTER VI

## THE FOUNDER OF MODERN BUSINESS

WHEN Jesus was twelve years old his father
and mother took him to the Feast at Jerusalem.

It was the big national vacation; even peasant
families saved their pennies and looked forward
to it through the year. Towns like Nazareth
were emptied of their inhabitants except for the
few old folks who were left behind to look after
the very young ones. Crowds of cheerful pilgrims filled the highways, laughing their way
across the hills and under the stars at night.

In such a mass of folk it was not surprising
that a boy of twelve should be lost. When Mary
and Joseph missed him on the homeward trip,
they took it calmly and began a search among
the relatives.

The inquiry produced no result. Some remembered having seen him in the Temple, but
no one had seen him since. Mary grew fright-

ened: where could he be? Back there in the city alone? Wandering hungry and tired through the friendless streets? Carried away by other travelers into a distant country? She pictured a hundred calamities. Nervously she and Joseph hurried back over the hot roads, through the suburbs, up through the narrow city streets, up to the courts of the Temple itself.

And there he was.

Not lost; not a bit worried. Apparently unconscious that the Feast was over, he sat in the midst of a group of old men, who were tossing questions at him and applauding the shrewd common sense of his replies. Involuntarily his parents halted—they were simple folk, uneasy among strangers and disheveled by their haste. But after all they *were* his parents, and a very human feeling of irritation quickly overcame their diffidence. Mary stepped forward and grasped his arm.

"Son, why hast thou thus dealt with us?" she demanded. "Behold thy father and I have sought thee sorrowing."

I wonder what answer she expected to receive. Did she ever know exactly what he was going to say: did any one in Nazareth quite understand this keen, eager lad, who had such curious moments of abstraction and was forever breaking out with remarks that seemed so far beyond his years?

He spoke to her now with deference, as always, but in words that did not dispel but rather added to her uncertainty.

"How is it that ye sought me?" he asked, "Wist ye not that I must be about my father's *business?*"

His father's business, indeed, as if that wasn't exactly where they wanted him to be. His father owned a prosperous carpenter shop in Nazareth, and that was the place for the boy, as he very well knew. She was on the point of saying so, but there was something in his look and tone that silenced her. She and Joseph turned and started out, and Jesus followed them—away from the temple and the city back to little Nazareth.

His hour of boyish triumph had not turned his head. He knew how thorough must be his preparation for any really successful work. A building can rise high into the air only as it has sunk its foundations deep into the earth; the part of a man's life which the world sees is effective in proportion as it rests upon solid work which is never seen. Instinctively he knew this. For eighteen years more he was content to remain in that country town—until his strength was at its summit; until he had done his full duty by his mother and the younger children. Until his hour had come.

But what interests us most in this one recorded incident of his boyhood is the fact that for the first time he defined the purpose of his career. He did not say, "Wist ye not that I must practise preaching?" or "Wist ye not that I must get ready to meet the arguments of men like these?" The language was quite different, and well worth remembering. "Wist ye not that I must be about my father's *business?*" he said. He thought of his life as *business*. What did he mean by business? To what extent are the principles by which he conducted his business applicable to ours? And if he were among us again, in our highly competitive world, would his business philosophy work?

On one occasion, you recall, he stated his recipe for success. It was on the afternoon when James and John came to ask him what promotion they might expect. They were two of the most energetic of the lot, called "Sons of Thunder," by the rest, being noisy and always in the midst of some sort of a storm. They had joined the ranks because they liked him, but with no very definite idea of what it was all about; and now they wanted to know where the enterprise was heading, and just what there would be in it for them.

"Master," they said, "we want to ask what plans you have in mind for us. You're going to need big men around you when you establish your kingdom; our ambition is to sit on either side of you, one on your right hand and the other on your left."

Who can object to that attitude? If a man fails to look after himself, certainly no one will look after him. If you want a big place, go ask for it. That's the way to get ahead.

Jesus answered with a sentence which sounds poetically absurd.

"Whosoever will be great among you, shall be your minister," he said, "and whosoever of you will be the chiefest, shall be servant of all."

A fine piece of rhetoric, now isn't it? Be a good servant and you will be great; be the best possible servant and you will occupy the highest possible place. Nice idealistic talk but utterly impractical; nothing to take seriously in a common sense world. That is just what men thought for some hundreds of years; and then, quite suddenly, Business woke up to a great discovery. You will hear that discovery proclaimed in every sales convention as something distinctly modern and up to date. It is emblazoned in the advertising pages of every magazine.

Look through those pages.

Here is the advertisement of an automobile

164

company, one of the greatest in the world. And why is it greatest? On what does it base its claim to leadership? On its huge factories and financial strength? They are never mentioned. On its army of workmen or its high salaried executives? You might read its advertisements for years without suspecting that it had either. No. "We are great because of our service," the advertisements cry. "We will crawl under your car oftener and get our backs dirtier than any of our competitors. Drive up to our service stations and ask for anything at all—it will be granted cheerfully. We serve; therefore we grow."

A manufacturer of shoes makes the same boast in other terms. "We put ourselves at your feet and give you everything that you can possibly demand." Manufacturers of building equipment, of clothes, of food; presidents of railroads and steamship companies; the heads of banks and investment houses—*all* of them tell the same story. "Service is what we are here for," they exclaim. They call it the "spirit of modern business"; they suppose, most of them, that it is something very new. But Jesus preached it more than nineteen hundred years ago.

One afternoon in a Pullman car the late George W. Perkins was talking about the reasons why men succeed and fail.

"I am amazed by some of the young men who ask me to use my influence to get them better positions or increases in salary," he said. "Such an attitude on their part shows an absolute failure to understand the fundamentals of success. In all the years that I was with the New York Life Insurance Company I never once asked what my salary was to be, or my title. None of us who made that Company ever wasted time over such questions. We had a vision of extending the Company's service throughout the world, of making it the finest, most useful institution of its kind. We made it that, and it made us rich."

That sounds sensible—good business sense. But how does this sound?

"If you're forever thinking about saving your

life," Jesus said, "you'll lose it; but the man who loses his life shall find it."

Because he said it and he was a religious teacher, because it's printed in the Bible, the world has dismissed it as high minded ethics but not hard headed sense. But look again! What did Perkins mean if it wasn't that he and his friends buried themselves in their great undertaking, literally lost their lives in it? And when they found their lives again, they were all of them bigger and richer than they had ever supposed they could be. Would such success have come to them if they had been careful about themselves? "We mustn't overdo this thing," they might have said. "This is a good Company and deserves to grow, but every man must look out for his own interests. Just what is there going to be in it for us?" With such an attitude they might have moved up to well paid positions; but never to outstanding success!

What did Henry Ford mean, one spring morning, when he tipped a kitchen chair back against the whitewashed wall of his tractor plant and talked about his career?

"Have you ever noticed that the man who starts out in life with a determination to make money, never makes very much?" he asked. It was rather a startling question; and without waiting for my comment he went on to answer it: "He may gather together a competence, of course, a few tens of thousands or even hundreds of thousands, but he'll never amass a really great fortune. But let a man start out in life to build something better and sell it cheaper than it has ever been built or sold before—let him have *that* determination, and give his whole self to it—and the money will roll in so fast that it will bury him if he doesn't look out.

"When we were building our original model, do you suppose that it was money we were thinking about? Of course we expected that it would be profitable, if it succeeded, but that wasn't in the front of our minds. We wanted to make a car so cheap that every family in the United States could afford to have one. So we worked morning, noon and night, until our muscles ached and our nerves were so ragged that it seemed as if we just couldn't stand it to hear any one mention the word automobile again. One night, when we were almost at the breaking point I said to the boys, 'Well, there's one consolation,' I said. 'Nobody can take this business away from us unless he's willing to work harder than we've worked.' And so far," he concluded with a whimsical smile, "nobody has been willing to do that."

What did Theodore N. Vail mean when he said that only once in his life did he set out with the deliberate intention of making money—that all the rest of his fortune had come from work which so gripped him that he forgot about the money? The one occasion to which he referred was his trip to South America where he found a mine that did prove profitable, and doubtless still is. He made that trip because he had lost all his money in an effort to establish a big central heating plant in Boston—to give people better warmth, as he had already helped to give them better communication. The heating plant failed, and he paid its debts with the South

American mine. But the bulk of his fortune came from the achievement for which he will always be remembered—the establishment of the American Telephone and Telegraph Company. To that great enterprise he gave everything he had—"threw his life into it," as we say—"lost his life in it," as Jesus said. And it gave him back larger and richer life, and a fortune and immortality.

"Whosoever shall compel thee to go a mile," said Jesus, "go with him twain."

Which means, I take it, "do more than is required of you, do twice as much." Another startling bit of business advice. Where will a man ever get, you ask, if he delivers twice as much as he is paid to deliver? The answer is that unless he's a fool he will probably get to and stay at the top. I remember once traveling from Chicago to New York on the Twentieth Century Limited. We were due in the Grand Central Station at nine-forty, a nice leisurely hour, and three of us who were traveling together decided to make a comfortable morning of it. We got out of our berths at a quarter after eight, shaved and dressed and half an hour later were making our way back to the dining-car.

A door to one of the drawing-rooms was open, and as we walked by we could hardly keep from looking in. The bed in the room had been made up long since; a table stood between the windows, and at the table, buried in work, was a man whose face the newspapers have made familiar to every one. He had been Governor of New York, a Justice of the Supreme Court, a candidate for the Presidency of the United States, and was—at the time—practising law and reputed to be earning much more than a hundred thousand dollars a year.

My companions and I were young men; he was well along in middle life. We were poor and unknown; he was rich and famous. We were doing all that was required of us. We were up and dressed and would be ready for business when the train pulled in at a little before ten. But this man, of whom nothing was actually required, was doing far more. I thought to myself as we passed on to our leisurely breakfast, "That explains him; now I understand Hughes."

I have several times been in the offices of J. P. Morgan and Company after six o'clock in the evening. I remember vividly the mental picture which I once had of what such a private banking house must be—the partners coming down in limousines at eleven and leaving at three, after having given their nonchalant approval to a million dollar deal. But on the occasion of one of the visits to which I refer the offices were closed. The clerks, and assistants and even the elevator men had gone, leaving only night-watchmen. Night-watchmen, *and* some of the partners. There seem to be always lights in the partners' offices no matter what the hour. Of the office force it is required that they travel the one mile which lies between nine o'clock in the morning and five o'clock at night. But the partners travel the second mile; have always traveled it all their lives; and are partners *because* they have.

Here is another business principle, seemingly equally impracticable.

Remember the words of the Lord Jesus how he said, *"It is more blessed to give than to receive."*

We came perilously near to losing those words. They are not recorded in any one of the four Gospels. Matthew, Mark, Luke and John all forgot them. "All very nice to talk about giving instead of getting," thought Matthew perhaps. "It may work in religion, but it's no good in the tax collecting business." "A splendid thought," John may have said to himself, "a very noble sentiment, but not quite practical in the fishing industry." Maybe they imagined that the Master had made a mistake, or that they had heard him incorrectly. At any rate they all passed over the saying. But Paul did not. He who had abandoned a social position and an assured career for the service of the Galilean, he who had given more than any of them, *he* heard the words and remembered. He understood.

Are they empty words? Do they bring destruction upon a business which regards them seriously? Is a man a fool to let them be a guiding influence in his life? I talked one day with H. G. Wells after his *Outline of History* had appeared. I said:

"You have stood upon a mountain and viewed the whole panorama of human progress. You have seen the captains and the kings, the princes and the prophets, the scientists and the adventurers, the millionaires and the dreamers—all the billions of human atoms that have lived and loved and struggled their little hour upon the earth. In this vast army what heads rise above the common level? Among all those who have fought for fame, *who* have actually achieved it? What half dozen men among them all deserve to be called great?"

He turned the question over in his mind for a day or two, and then gave me a list of six names, with his reasons for each. An extraordinary list!

Jesus of Nazareth

Buddha

# FOUNDER OF MODERN BUSINESS

Asoka

Aristotle

Roger Bacon

Abraham Lincoln

Think of the thousands of emperors who have battled for fame; who have decreed themselves immortal, and fashioned their immortality into monuments of brick and stone. Yet there is only one emperor, Asoka, on the list; and he is there not because of his victories but because he voluntarily abandoned war, after his success, and devoted himself to the betterment of his millions of subjects. Think of the hosts who have struggled for wealth, fretting over figures, denying their generous instincts, cheating and grasping and worrying. Yet no millionaire is on the list, excepting again Asoka. Who sat on the throne in Rome, when Jesus of Nazareth hung on the cross? Who ruled the hosts of Persia when Aristotle thought and taught? Who was King of England when Roger Bacon laid the foundations of modern scientific research?

# THE MAN NOBODY KNOWS

The tumult and the shouting dies,
The captains and the kings depart.

And when the historian, looking over the field
where they contended for the prize, seeks for
something which has endured, he finds the message of a teacher, the dream of a scientist, the
vision of a seer. "These six men stood on the
corners of History," said Wells in his pic-
turesque way. "Events hinged on them. The
current of human thought was freer and clearer
because they had lived and worked. They took
little from the world and left it much. They did
not get; they gave; and, in the giving, gained
eternal influence."

In our own country, in Monticello, in Virginia, an American statesman lies buried. He
was Secretary of State, Minister to France,
President of the United States; yet his epitaph
makes reference to none of these honors. It
reads:

Here was buried
Thomas Jefferson
Author
of the Declaration of American Independence

of the Statute of Virginia
for Religious Freedom
and Father of the
University of Virginia

The offices that he held are forgotten on the stone, as they will be eventually forgotten by all but the historian; he desired to be remembered only by what he gave. And he has his wish.

Somewhere in his *Essays* Emerson has a sentence to this effect: "See how the mass of men worry themselves into nameless graves, while here and there a great unselfish soul forgets himself into immortality." A fine thought, finely phrased; but Jesus thought it first.

So we have the main points of his business philosophy:

1. Whoever will be great must render great service.

2. Whoever will find himself at the top must be willing to lose himself at the bottom.

3. The big rewards come to those who travel the second, undemanded mile.

Judas would have sneered at all this. Not a bad fellow at heart, he had the virtues and the weaknesses of the small bore business man. He was "hard-boiled," and proud of it; he "looked out for Number One." It was no easy job being treasurer for a lot of idealists, Judas would have you know. He held the bag and gave every cent a good tight squeeze before he let it pass. When the grateful woman broke her box of costly ointment over Jesus' feet the other disciples thought it was fine, but he knew better. "Pretty wasteful business," he grumbled to himself. The big talk of the others about "thrones" and "kingdoms" and "victory" did not fool him; he could read a balance sheet, and he knew that the jig was up. So he made his private little deal with the priests, probably supposing that Jesus would be arrested, reproved and warned not to preach in Jerusalem again. "I will get mine and retire," he said to himself. Said Jesus, "I, if I be lifted up (on the cross; that is to say, if I lose my life) will draw all men to me." Each made his decision and received his reward.

We have quoted some men of conspicuous success, but the same sound principles apply to every walk of life. Great progress will be made in the world when we rid ourselves of the idea that there is a difference between *work* and *religious work*. We have been taught that a man's daily business activities are selfish, and that only the time which he devotes to church meetings and social service activities is consecrated. Ask any ten people what Jesus meant by his "Father's business," and nine of them will answer "preaching." To interpret the words in this narrow sense is to lose the real significance of his life. It was not to preach that he came into the world; nor to teach; nor to heal. These are all departments of his Father's business, but the business itself is far larger, more inclusive. For if human life has any significance it is this—that God has set going here an experiment to which all His resources are committed. He seeks to develop perfect human beings, superior to circumstance, victorious over Fate. No single kind of human talent or effort can be spared if the experiment is to succeed. The race must be fed and clothed and housed and transported, as well as preached to, and taught and healed. Thus *all* business is his Father's business. All work is worship; all useful service prayer. And whoever works wholeheartedly at any worthy calling is a co-worker with the Almighty in the great enterprise which He has initiated but which He can never finish without the help of men.

It is one thing to talk about success, and quite another thing to win it. Jesus spoke of crowns and died on a cross. He talked of his kingdom, and ended his days amid the jeers and taunts of his enemies. "He was in all points tempted like as we are," says the Epistle to the Hebrews. We have read it often, heard it read oftener, but we have never believed it, of course. . . . The conception of his character which Theology has given us makes any such idea impossible. He was born differently from the rest of us, Theology insists. He did not belong among us at all, but came down from Heaven on a brief visit, spent a few years in reproving men for their mistakes, died and went back to Heaven again. A hollow bit of stage-play. What chance for temptation in such a career? How can an actor go wrong when his whole part is written and learned in advance?

It is frightfully hard to free the mind from the numbing grip of ancient creeds. But let us make the effort. Let us touch once more the high spots in this finest, most exalted success story, considering now the perils and crises of success.

He was not at all sure where he was going when he laid down his tools and turned his back on the carpenter shop—unless we can believe this, his struggle ceases to be "in all points" like our own; for each of us has to venture on Life as on to an uncharted sea. Something inside him carried him forward—the something which has whispered to so many small town boys that there is a place for them in the world which lies beyond the hills. He went to John to be baptized and for a while John's influence molded him. He, too, retired into the wilderness and there met the *first* crisis of his career. When he emerged he had formed his own plan for his work; asceticism and denunciation, he knew, were not the role for him.

His first success was swift beyond all expectations. Out of the Temple, shrieking and cursing, went the money-changers, while the crowd cheered his name to the echo. That night the whole city was stirred by the story. When he left, at the end of the feast, and went back into his own north country, he found that his fame had preceded him. Crowds flocked to hear him talk; news of his deeds of healing traveled ahead of him everywhere. His vision of his work began to take definite shape. He would restore the self-respect of the people, abolishing the rule of formalism, and establishing a fresh, glorious conception of the Fatherhood of God, and the brotherhood of man. It all seemed so natural, so easy, there in the warm sunshine of Galilee with the responsive faces of the multitude turned eagerly toward him. The year or year and a half that followed were filled with the joy of increasing reputation and success. Apparently there was not a single cloud in the sky.

But there were people in Jerusalem with whose private affairs his ideas would seriously interfere. He was not left long in doubt as to their attitude. Incensed at his cleansing of the Temple, they sent their spies into the north country to report his movements and made every effort to turn the crowds away. Perhaps at first he had hope of winning even his enemies to his teaching—so altogether simple and satisfying his gospel seemed to him. If so, the hope soon vanished. Opposition crystallized; it made itself felt in every audience he addressed, in every town he visited. Reluctantly he had to face the fact that the time was coming when he must compromise or fight. It was with this realization that he faced a second and a greater crisis.

He had crossed the lake one day in a little boat to get away from the crowds; but they were too quick for him. Running around the end of the lake, and gathering recruits as they ran, they waited for him at the landing place—more than five thousand strong. He was tired, and wanted a chance to rest and think. But here were the people, pathetically eager, and he "had compassion on them." So he sat down among them and went on with his teaching until the day was almost over. Then, at last, the disciples came, hardly concealing their tired petulance, and demanded that he send them away.

"But they have made a long trip and have been with us all day without food," he replied. "We must feed them before they go."

The disciples regarded him with blank amazement.

"Feed them—on what?" they demanded. "We have no money, and even if we had there are more than five thousand in the crowd!"

Jesus apparently did not hear them.

"Have them sit down," he commanded. "Gather up whatever food you can find and bring it here to me."

Doubtingly, but too well trained to argue, the disciples did as they were told. They arranged the crowd in companies of fifty and a hundred, collected the little supply of food which the more prudent members had brought. and laid the collection at his feet. He lifted his eyes to heaven, blessed the food, ordered it redistributed and somehow the people ate and were satisfied.

Just what happened in the moment when the food was laid before him is an impenetrable mystery; but there is no doubt at all as to what took place afterward. It was the event for which the people had waited, the unmistakable sign! Moses had fed their fathers on manna in the wilderness; here was one who likewise called on Heaven, and supplied their wants. Surely he was the son of David, long foretold, who would overthrow the rule of their conquerors and restore the throne to Jerusalem!

Joyously they shouted the news back and forth. The day of deliverance had come; the tyranny of the Romans was about to end. Their enthusiasm carried them to their feet—fifty in this group, a hundred in that; almost as if by magic they found themselves organized. They were an army and had not realized it. Right there on the field they were enough to outnumber the garrison in Jerusalem; but they were only a nucleus of the host that would gather to their banners, once their southward march was formed. If they were five thousand now, they would be fifty thousand, perhaps a hundred thousand then. A wild enthusiasm seized upon them; shouting his name at the top of their voices they surged forward toward the little hill where he stood—

And then—

He had foreseen their purpose, and even while they were perfecting their plan, doubt had raged through his spirit with the force of a tempest. Why not accept their nomination? Why not be their king? It would mean an alteration in his program, to be sure—a surrender of his vision of spiritual leadership. And yet it *might* not be such a surrender, after all. Solomon had been king, and a great spiritual leader; David had been king and had written the nation's highest ideals into his Psalms. He himself was better balanced than David, wiser than Solomon— why not?

It was as splendid a picture as ever stirred the

pulses of an ambitious man. For only an instant Jesus allowed his eyes to rest on it. Then he saw the other picture—the vast dumb multitudes of men, his brothers and sisters, the blind being led by the blind, their souls squeezed dry of vision and hope by the machinery of formalism. He saw generations born and die in spiritual servitude which nothing could end except the Truth that he had come to declare. To put himself at the head of this army of fanatical patriots would be perhaps to risk his life and his message with it. But worse than the possibility of failure was the probability of success. To be king of the Jews would mean a lifetime spent in the defense of his throne and title, a lifetime of bloodshed and intrigue, while his message remained unspoken. Living, he would give his people only a semblance of national life; dying, he would leave them to be re-enslaved by the Roman power. And the Truth which he had come to declare, which was capable of continuing its work of emancipation throughout the world so long as time should last, would be traded for

a glittering crown and an empty name. In a
flash he saw it all and made his decision. Even
as the multitude surged forward, he gave a few
crisp orders to his disciples and disappeared.

The Gospel story puts the dramatic climax
into a single sentence:

> *Jesus, therefore, perceiving that they were
> about to come and take him by force to make
> him king, withdrew again into the mountain
> himself alone.*

In that hour of crisis he proved his right to be
the silent partner in every modern business; to
sit at the head of every directors' table. There
is no mere theorizing in his words; he speaks out
of what he himself has proved. If he says that
a man's work is more eternally important than
any title, he has a right to speak. He himself
refused the highest title. If he says that there
are things more vital than merely making
money, let no one question his authority. He
was handed the wealth of a nation and handed
it back again. Idealist he is, but there is nothing in the whole hard world so practical as his

ideals. "There is a success which is greater than wealth or titles," he says. "It comes through making your work an instrument of greater service, and larger living to your fellow men and women. *This* is my Father's business and he needs your help."

He told one business story which should be published every year in all magazines of business, all trade papers, all house organs. It concerned a certain rich man whose enterprises prospered beyond all his expectations. His land "brought forth plentifully," so much so that he said to himself: "What shall I do, because I have no room where to bestow my fruits?"

And he said: "This will I do; I will pull down my barns and build greater; and there will I bestow all my fruits and my goods."

And I will say to my soul, "Soul, thou hast much goods laid up for many years; take thine ease, eat, drink and be merry."

But God said, "Thou fool, this night thy soul shall be required of thee."

The poor fool had regarded his business as nothing but a means of escape from business.

He had hoarded his wealth, denying every generous impulse; spent his health, forfeiting every chance for wholesome enjoyment; sacrificed the joy of living for a selfish satisfaction that he hoped was coming when he had made his pile. And Fate laughed in his face. He thought he had provided for every contingency, but the one great Event which is always unexpected came like a thief in the night and found him unprepared. . . .

With that business anecdote should be published another, which is also a tragedy. It concerns the little hotel in Bethlehem, "the inn."

The mother of Jesus of Nazareth knocked at its doors and could not come in. It might have sheltered the greatest event in human history, and it lost its chance.

Why? Why was Jesus born in a stable? Because the people in the inn were vicious or hostile? Not in the least. The inn was full, that was all; every room was taken by folk who had affairs to attend to and money to spend. It was busy.

# FOUNDER OF MODERN BUSINESS

There was no "room in the inn."

Men's lives are sometimes like that inn.

You know a man whose heart is broken because his son is a fool. Yet deep within himself he knows that the fault is his own. All through the formative years of the boy's development, he never gave him any time. Not that he didn't love the boy; but he was busy. There was no room for family life; and his son is a fool.

You know men whose health is gone; men whose taste for reading and music and art is gone. Men who have literally no interests in life beyond the office which has become a mere treadmill whereon their days are ground away.

In the process of being successful they have sacrificed success. Never once forgetting themselves they have forgotten everything else. This is not Jesus' idea of what a life should be. He, who refused to turn aside from his business to become a king, was never too busy to turn aside for a sick man, a friend, a little child. He never forgot that one night his mother had stood on a threshold where there was no welcome.

# THE MAN NOBODY KNOWS

The threshold of the little inn in Bethlehem. It was so busy that the greatest event in history knocked at its doors

—and could not come in.

# CHAPTER VII

## THE MASTER

So WE come up to the end. To the final tests
of a man's living—

How does he bear disappointment?

How does he die?

For two years it seemed almost certain that
Jesus would prevail. He himself was sure of it.
We have marked the dramatic success with
which his work began. We have watched the
crowds flock about him in the market-place; we
have heard the cheers that greeted his victories
over shrewd antagonists, and the murmured awe
when a sick man rose and walked. Reports of
his triumphs preceded him everywhere so that
men competed for the honor of being his host,
and there was friendliness in his audiences that
made almost anything seem possible. And why
not? If, by accepting his message, men could be

lifted up, transformed into sons of God, heirs of eternity, why should any be so stubborn or so foolish as to oppose? Surely such Truth *must* conquer.

If you read the story carefully you can see how his tone and manner grew in confidence. In hours of exalted communion he stood face to face with God, felt his own sonship, knew that he could lift the hearts of men as no other had ever lifted them. The knowledge thrilled him with ecstasy. "I am the Way," he cried, and he called on his friends to free themselves, to cast their burdens upon the Lord, to believe more, rejoice more, expect more of God. Those who listened in those days were profoundly impressed. Even the most callous yielded grudging admiration. "Never man so spake," said they. As for the multitude, its enthusiasm would brook no half-way measures. They would take him by force and make him king.

Then came the change.

*His home town was first to turn against him.* Picture, if you will, the enthusiasm with which he planned his visit to it. Nazareth was little and despised, a jest among the wits of the day. It had produced no great men, been the scene of no historic achievement. Jesus knew all this. Those familiar streets and faces were often in his memory. When he healed a sick man in Capernaum, it pleased him to think that the report would be carried back to Nazareth. When he drove the plunderers from the Temple he realized that, in the fame which had come to him, his home town would have a share. "Jesus of Nazareth," the world called him, linking its name with his. He had lifted the little village out of obscurity. And now, in the height of his glory, he was going back.

Did he arrive in the dusk and slip almost unnoticed through the streets to his mother's house? Perhaps she was in the kitchen, and hearing that footstep which she could never mistake, she ran and threw her arms around his neck.

"Jesus," she cries, patting his cheek and looking up at him with glistening eyes, "Jesus, my boy, my boy!"

Hearing the name his brothers and sisters come hurrying from other parts of the house. All sorts of reports have drifted back—almost unbelievable reports. Every day the gossips of the village have stopped them to ask whether a letter or a message has come.

"Seems to be doing great things," said the gossips with ill-concealed envy. "Hope he doesn't try to go too far," they said in tones which revealed all too clearly their real hope that he *would* go too far, and come to grief.

Against cynicism and innuendo his brothers had stood their ground proudly. He *was* doing great things, they insisted; the reports were not a bit exaggerated. Some day he would come back and show them all; they would wish then that they had believed. . . . And now he *was* back. Healthy he looked, and confident; but not otherwise different. They were a bit disappointed and he felt it. They hardly knew what it was, but they had expected that he would be somehow bigger, or better dressed, or tagged with some outward sign of authority. . . . With forced enthusiasm they bustled about, asking him questions, praising his good looks; but through it all, ran a note of restraint.

"Come now, you must get to bed early," his mother may have said. "They will all be wanting to see you at the synagogue to-morrow."

So he went up to the room, his old room, alone. The home coming was not quite what he had dreamed. They loved him; they were proud of him, but they doubted—that was clear enough. And they dreaded the test that must come next day.

He awoke refreshed and heartened. Some neighbors dropped in after breakfast, for the report of his arrival had spread quickly through the little town. When he and his mother reached the door of the synagogue a crowd was waiting outside. They returned his greeting with a mixture of regard and curiosity, and pushed promptly through the door behind him, filling the little room full. There was much whispering and craning of necks. He made his way to the front of the room, picked up the roll of the prophet Isaiah, turned around toward them and smiled.

Instantly all his illusions vanished. Instead of sympathetic understanding there was only cynicism on those faces. The old woman, his neighbor, whom he had planned to heal, was sitting prominently in front. She was willing to take a chance on anything, for she had been a long time sick; but her look was less a hope than a challenge. The substantial men of the town settled solidly in their appointed seats, and dared him with their hard eyes to try his tricks on *them!* "You may have caused a stir in Capernaum," they seemed to say, "but little old Nazareth isn't so slow. We know you. You're no prophet; you're just the son of Joseph the carpenter, and you can't fool us!"

Slowly he opened the roll and in tones that stirred them in spite of themselves he began to read:

The Spirit of the Lord is upon me
Because he anointed me to preach of good tidings to the poor,

198

He hath sent me to proclaim release to the cap-
tives,
And recovery of sight to the blind;
To set at liberty them that are bruised,
And proclaim the acceptable year of the Lord.

He closed the book and handed it back to the
attendant. "This day hath this Scripture been
fulfilled in your ears," he said simply. There
was an ominous silence in the synagogue. "The
eyes of all were fastened upon Him." He knew
what they were thinking; they wanted him to do
some mighty work such as he had done in Capernaum. But he knew also the uselessness of trying. The scorn, the ignorant self-sufficiency
were miracle proof. They would never receive
him; never be proud of him. They merely
wanted him to exhibit himself and they hoped
that he would fail. "No prophet is acceptable
in his own country," he said to them sadly.
"Elijah did his greatest works in a foreign city;
Elisha could accomplish nothing big until he got
beyond the borders of his home." With a look
of soul-weariness he turned to leave.

Then the storm broke. All the pent-up envy of the little town for one who has dared to outgrow it, gathered itself into a roar. They surged forward hurrying him through the main street to the edge of a precipice where they would have thrown him over. But the wrath which had been sufficient to conceive his destruction grew suddenly impotent when he turned and faced them. They shrank back, and before they could reform their purpose, he had passed through the midst of them and was on his way. In his ears sounded the buzz of malicious comment, but he was too heart-sick to look back. From henceforth Capernaum became "his own city." Nazareth, the home of his youth, the dwelling place of his boyhood friends and neighbors, had given its verdict.

He had come unto his own, and his own received him not.

*His brothers deserted him.* We ought not to blame them too much, perhaps. No man is a hero to his valet; and the near relatives of any great man, who have lived with him through the familiar experiences of every-day life, must be always a little mystified by the world's worship. The brothers of Jesus had been witnesses of his defeat, and were left behind by him to bear the ignominy of it. How the sardonic laughter must have rung in their ears! How endlessly the wits must have cracked their jokes about that morning in the synagogue. . . . These home town sneers were bad enough, but the reports that came back from other towns threw the simple unimaginative family into a panic. It was said that he made seditious speeches; that he claimed to have a special relationship to God; that he utterly disregarded the code of the Pharisees and denounced them openly before the crowds. Such conduct could mean only one thing. He would get himself into jail, and his relatives with him. Hence the members of his family who should have been his best helpers spent their energy in the effort to get him to go farther away from home. Once when the feast of tabernacles was being celebrated in Jerusalem, they urged him to "go up" to "depart hence" and taunted him, saying that if he could really do all that he claimed, the place for him to make his reputation was at the capital. Anything to get him out of Galilee. They were all unsafe while he stayed near them—so they thought.

"For even his brethren did not believe in him."

He was teaching one day in Capernaum to a crowd that hung spellbound on his words, when suddenly an interruption occurred. A messenger pushed through the audience to tell him that his mother and brothers were outside and insisted on speaking to him right away. A quick look of pain shot across his fine face. He knew why they had come; they had been sending him threats of their coming for weeks. They had made up their minds that he was just a little bit out of his head, and they were determined to shut him up in an asylum before his extravagances should ruin them all. He drew himself up to his full height and pointing to his disciples turned to the messenger:

"My mother and brethren?" he repeated. "Behold these who believe on me, *they* are my mother and my brethren."

They *were* indeed his real kindred and many
times they proved themselves worthy of the
name; but even their devotion could not entirely
remove the hurt.  When later he had his brief
hour of triumph, when the crowds flung their
garments into the streets before him and shouted
their "hosannas," even then his heart must have
been sore at the thought that in all that multitude there was not one of the brothers for whom
he had sacrificed so much of his youth.  A warm
hand-clasp from one of them would have meant
more than all the high homage of the multitude.
But they were far away, still ashamed of the relationship, still regarding him as well meaning
but not quite sane.

*His best friend died doubting him.*  To that
friend, John the Baptist, he owed his initial success.  John had introduced him to the people;
his first disciples had come because John pointed
him out as a greater prophet than himself.  The
two men were entirely unlike in character and
method.  John was austere, harsh, denunciatory
--a lonely spirit, dwelling apart.  Jesus was

cheerful, friendly, never happier than when in a crowd. John laid down for his disciples a rigid program of ceremonies and fasts; Jesus disregarded forms and encouraged his disciples to disregard them. He recognized that he and John must do their work in different ways, but it had not occurred to him that their differences would ever loosen the bond of friendship. He was cut to the quick, therefore, when two messengers came from John with a wistful, doubting question:

"Are you *really* a prophet, as I told people that you are?" John asked. "Instead of fasting you banquet. Instead of calling on men to abjure pleasure, you share their pleasures. Are you the hope of the world, as I believed you to be, or must we look for another?"

Very tenderly, but sadly, Jesus sent back his reply: "Go tell John what you have seen and heard," he said, "how the blind see, lepers are cleansed and the poor have the good news preached to them."

It was a wonderful answer, but did it convince

his friend? A few weeks later, in the dungeon of Herod's castle, John paid the last great penalty for his idealism and courage. Jesus, when he heard of it, "withdrew into the hills alone." His closest friend and first adherent had gone out—a sacrifice to the selfishness of a social order which he himself was fighting. In that heart-breaking event he saw an omen for himself. They who had been strong enough to murder John would one day destroy him also. It was a bitter blow to his visions of success. When he returned from the hills there was a new seriousness in his face, a harder note in his teachings. He saw at the end of his path the shadow of the cross. And his heart was heavy because the friend who ought to have understood him best, had misunderstood him and died in doubt.

*The people deserted him.* When last we caught a glimpse of them they were cheering his name beside the lake, seeking to force him to be their king. He eluded them and retired into the mountain to think and pray. It must have been a dramatic moment when he reappeared. Only a single "Yes" was needed and they would have lifted him on their shoulders and borne him in triumph to the city gates. Hushed and expectant they waited for his answer—and what an answer! "I am not come to restore the kingdom to Jerusalem," he cried. "Mine is a spiritual mission; I am the bread of life. You have cheered me because I fed you in the wilderness, but I tell you now that what I have come to give you is myself, that by knowing me you may know your Father."

They could not have been more stunned if he had struck their leaders across the face. What did he mean by this senseless mysticism, this talk about "the bread of life"? Hadn't they seen him heal the sick and conquer the Pharisees in debate —were not these signs that he was the leader, so long promised, who would rout the Romans and restore the throne of David? And now, when the hour was ripe, when they were ready to march, why this language which nobody could understand?

"The Jews therefore murmured concerning

him, because he said 'I am the bread that came down from Heaven.'" It was sacrilege or non-sense, one or the other. In either event it proved him an unsound leader. Gentiles might continue to follow him, if they chose, but his company was clearly no place for a self-respecting Jew.

Silently the cautious people slipped away, and afterward denied that they had ever had any-thing to do with him. Those who were more daring, or devoted, continued with him through the rest of the week, and on the Sabbath crowded into the synagogue where they knew that he would speak. The days had given him time to reconsider and compose his thoughts; perhaps now he would make a reasonable reply to their hopes. But there was no compromise in his message that day. Again he repeated his seemingly senseless talk about the "bread of life." It destroyed the last hope of those who had looked to him for the deliverance of Israel. "These are hard sayings," they protested, "who can understand them?" And then the note of tragedy.

*"Upon this many of his disciples went back and walked with him no more."*

The tide had turned. He realized it clearly though the disciples could not. At every opportunity he sought to build up in them an increased sense of their responsibilities. He must "go into Jerusalem," he told them, "and suffer many things of the elders and chief priests and scribes, and be killed." They could not, would not believe it. Peter, hot-headed and enthusiastic, took him aside and rebuked him for what seemed a temporary loss of courage. "Be it far from thee, Lord," he exclaimed; "this shall never be unto thee." Generous loyal words, but they revealed an utter failure to appreciate the real situation. All hope of a revived and regenerated nation was gone; his one chance now for permanent influence was in welding his little group closer together, and sealing their union with his blood.

For the first time in his public work he forsook Palestine and led his wondering but still dutiful followers into the foreign cities of Tyre

and Sidon. The journey gave him a chance to
be alone with the twelve; and it was, in a small
way, a repetition of his earlier triumphs. These
foreign folk were friendly without ulterior mo-
tive. They cared nothing about the establishment of a throne in Jerusalem, or the possibility
of profit for themselves from his political triumph. They came to hear him because his words
thrilled them, because they felt their better
selves touched and made vibrant by the wonder
of his life.

He hated to leave these kindly strangers.
Much more he dreaded the thought of another
trip through Galilee. What a graveyard of high
hopes it was! Every road, every street corner,
almost every house and tree was alive with
memories of his success. Now he must pass each
one again, conscious that it might be the last
time, his heart weighed down with the thought
of high purposes that had brought no response,
and sacrifices seemingly in vain. Small wonder
that he cried out against Chorazin and Bethsaida and even his own loved Capernaum, the

cities for which he had done so much. "Woe unto you," he cried in his loneliness, "for if the mighty works which were done in you had been done in Tyre and Sidon they would have repented long ago, in sack-cloth and ashes."

But neither Bethsaida nor Capernaum had ears for him any longer. Some new novelty had taken hold of the public imagination. He had had his day; nothing more was to be expected from him. . . . So the spring and summer passed, and autumn came, bringing the feast of tabernacles, which he determined to celebrate in Jerusalem. It was a suicidal resolve. The report of his dwindling influence had been carried to the Temple clique which was emboldened by the information. There were spies in every crowd that listened to him; the echo of his smallest act flew to the capital; he could not hope to arrive outside the city walls without imminent danger of arrest. All this he knew but it did not weigh against his resolve. This might be his last feast. There would be visitors from all over the world, some of whom would surely take the seed of his message with them back to their homes. He must be true to his calling at whatever cost. So he went.

We catch one glimpse of him on the Temple steps, surrounded by a partly curious, partly antagonistic crowd. It was his chance to recapture a little of the popular favor, to speak a placating word that might open the way to reconciliation; but no such thought entered his mind. The time for defiance had come. "I have offered you the truth," he cried, "the truth that would make you free." And when they shouted that they were sons of Abraham and hence already free, he replied that they were no children of Abraham, but "children of the devil."

They would have killed him then and there, but their courage failed. After all he had still a considerable following, and it was better to wait. Give him rope and he would tangle himself inextricably. Every speech was alienating somebody. When the time was ripe they would seize him—perhaps at the next feast, if in the meantime he had not entirely discredited himself and disappeared. So they argued among themselves, and he went back once more into his Galilee.

Just for a moment, in the next spring, there seemed to be a renewed popular interest. The crowds flocked around in the old familiar way; the disciples noted it joyously. "The multitudes come together to him again," they exclaimed and at once their hopes were busy with new visions of his success. But dismay followed fast. Against their ardent protest he carried them off into close retirement. They were restless, lonely, distressed at the high handed fashion in which he turned away supporters. Was it necessary to be so harsh with the Pharisees? After all there were many estimable men among them whose contributions would have been very helpful. Why should he have ridiculed them out of his company? Why tell people that their precious ritual was less acceptable to God than the cry for mercy of an untaught publican? Why slight their ready hospitality in favor of an outcast like Zacchæus. His little group of friends were still groping for a clear vision of message and purposes when for the last time he led them down to Jerusalem and the final feast.

The one week of his life which everybody knows is the last week. Hence we pass over it in this little book. It began with the triumphant shouts of "hosanna"; it ended with the blood-thirsty cries of "crucify." Between the first morning of triumph and the last hours of mortal agony it witnessed his finest verbal victories over his opponents. Never were his nerves more steady, his courage higher, his mind more keen. Deliberately he piled up the mountain of hatred, knowing that it would kill him, but determined that there should be no doubt through the ages as to *what* he had stood for, and *why* he had to die. Every man who loves courageous manhood ought to read these final chapters at least once a year. Any attempt to abridge or paraphrase them would result in failure or worse. We pass over them in reverent silence, stopping only for a glimpse of the three most wonderful scenes.

First the final supper on that cool, quiet Thursday night. He knew that he should never

meet with the disciples around the table again.
All the memories of the three great years must
have crowded into his mind as the meal progressed. How often they had sat together under
a tree beside the lake, sharing the fish that their
own nets had caught. How they had enjoyed
that first meal at Cana, when he turned the
water into wine. What a glorious afternoon it
was when he fed five thousand, and the shouts
of gladness echoed back and forth among the
hills. And this was the end. His relatives had
turned their backs on him; his home town had
scorned his advances; his best friend had died
doubting; the people had turned away, and his
enemies were about to triumph—is there any
other leader who would have stood forth un-
broken by such blows? What was *his* attitude?
Complaint? Fault finding? Weak railing at
his own misfortunes or the wilful wickedness of
men? See, he rises in his place. He speaks, this
proud young man who had refused to be a king
and now is to die with common thieves. And
*these* are his words:

# THE MASTER

*Let not your heart be troubled . . .*
*I have overcome the world.*

There is nothing in history so majestic!
Already one of his disciples had slipped away
to betray him. That very night the soldiers
would take him, bind him, throw him into
prison. The priests and Pharisees whom he had
taunted would have their turn to taunt him now.
He would be harried through the streets like a
hunted thing, the butt of every corner loafer's
jest. All this he anticipated, and with the vision
of it fresh before his mind, he lifted his head and
looked beyond, into the far distant ages. "Be
of good cheer," he said to them, in tones whose
splendor thrills us even now. "I have overcome
the world!"

They went out into the garden where so many
of their happy hours had been spent. The very
air was fragrant with their most sacred con-
fidences. Under this tree they had gathered for
worship, while the setting sun gilded the towers
of the city; in the waters of that brook they had
found refreshment; to left and right of them the

very stones cried out in heartrending reminder of the days that were gone. Even at that hour it was not too late for him to have saved his life. Suppose he had said to himself: "I have delivered my message faithfully, and it is no use. Judas has gone already to bring the soldiers; they will be here in half an hour. Why should I stay and die? It is only eighteen miles to Jericho, bright moonlight and down hill all the way. Our friend Zacchæus will be glad to see us. We can reach his house by daylight, rest tomorrow, cross the Jordan and do useful work the rest of our lives. The disciples can fish; I can open a carpenter shop, and teach in a quiet way. I have done everything that could be expected of me. Why not?"

It was all perfectly possible. The rulers in Jerusalem would have been glad to be rid of him on such terms. He might so easily have continued on down the hill to peace and a comfortable old age—and oblivion. It was the last great temptation and decisively he dismissed it. He walked a little ahead in silence, followed by the

eleven—for Judas was with them no longer—
and coming to a quiet place, left them while he
went away for his last hour of high communion
with his Father, God.

A few minutes later he returned to find them
sleeping. Even so short a vigil had proved too
heavy for their feebleness. In the hour of his
greatest need there was no help from them.
Again he went away, his spirit torn with agony.
He was young, thirty-three; he did not want to
die. He cried out to God that the cup might pass
from his lips; that he might have time to sweep
away the charges of blasphemy and evil which
his enemies had heaped upon him; time to build
up the fragile stuff of his little band on whom
the whole future of his message must depend;
time to round out the full measure of his years
and influence. So he prayed, and coming back,
found them again asleep.

This time he did not disturb them. The high
tide of his revolt had subsided; the courage
which had never deserted him throughout the
three years cleared his soul, steadied his muscles.

217

"If it be not thy will that this cup pass from me," he prayed again, "then, Father, thy will be done."

It was the victory chant after the battle. With the calm peace of the conqueror he could make ready for the end. He had not long to wait. The soldiers were already at the entrance of the garden. From his vantage point on the side of the hill he could mark the progress of their torches across the brook and up the path. The clang of their arms rang jarringly through the trees; rough exclamations smote the evening air like profanity in a temple. He waited until the armed men stumbled into his presence and then, rising, stood before them.

"Whom seek ye?" he demanded.

Startled, awed, they could only mumble his name.

"Jesus of Nazareth."

"I am he," he answered proudly.

They had expected angry denunciation, perhaps resistance; these they understood and could cope with. But such calm, such dignity were beyond the boundaries of their experience. Involuntarily they gave way and, rough veterans as they were, some of them "fell to the ground." It was a tribute, silent but magnificent.

"I told you," he repeated calmly, "that I am he." And then, his thought rebounding at once to those who had shared his triumphs and his sacrifices through the years, "If therefore ye seek me let these others go their way." But he had no need to think of the disciples' safety. Already they had made their swift escape—the last of the deserters—

—first his home town
—then his best friend
—then his relatives
—then the crowd
—finally the eleven.

All who had stood at his side had gone and left him to face his fate alone.

On a barren hill beyond the city walls they nailed his perfect body to the cross. Two robbers were crucified with him. It was over. The rabble had sickened quickly of its revenge and scattered; his friends were hiding; the soldiers were busy casting lots for his garments. There was nothing left of the external influences which fire men's imaginations or grip their loyalty. Surely the victory of his enemies was complete; he could do no miracle there, hanging on a cross.

And yet—

"Jesus." It was the voice of one of the robbers. "Jesus," he says painfully, "remember me, *when thou comest into thy kingdom!*"

Read that, oh men, and bow your heads. You who have let yourself picture him as weak, as a man of sorrows, uninspiring, glad to die. There have been leaders who could call forth enthusiasm when their fortunes ran high. But he, when his enemies had done their worst, so bore himself that a crucified felon looked into his dying eyes and saluted him as king.